NO REGRETS ON SUNDAY

THE SEVEN-DAY PLAN TO CHANGE YOUR LIFE

NO REGRETS ON SUNDAY

PETER HAWKINS

Vermilion
LONDON

Designed and set by seagulls.net
Illustrations by Alexander McGregor

Printed in the UK by CPI Group (UK) Ltd, Croydon, CR0 4YY

ISBN 9780091947408

To buy books by your favourite authors and register for offers visit
www.randomhouse.co.uk

To three precious gifts – my sons James, Matthew and Christopher, who I love dearly and hope will have no regrets on Sunday.

contents

preface

The germ of the idea for this book was planted in my mind when I was 17 years old. At this young age I was diagnosed with macular degeneration, a rare eye disorder which, among other things, doctors told me meant that I would never be able to drive a car, even if I was wearing glasses. It was a massive blow at the time – seeming to deprive me of one of the first milestones of becoming an independent adult.

Month after month I had to go to the pub with my mates to celebrate them all, one by one, passing their driving test and watch them head out to buy their first car. Feeling different from everyone else, I used to walk home feeling frustrated, and then I would go up to my bedroom and pray that everybody else would fail their driving test! (Apologies if you failed first time – I didn't mean it.) It took three years of feeling sorry for myself before the penny dropped. When my sister Kathryn passed her test, I suddenly realised that the more people who passed their test the more people there were who could drive me around, which meant the more beers I could have that they couldn't! It was at this 'tipping point' that I realised that my biggest disability wasn't my eyesight, it was the way I was coping with the loss of it.

In a eureka moment I realised that we all have a choice: 'When the wind blows, some people build walls, others build windmills.' The winds of change are blowing faster than ever before in our lives. We can resist them and build walls, or we can use them to release our full potential by building windmills.

Fifteen years ago I joined forces with a like-minded friend, Helen Wakefield, and together we have embraced a growing family of colleagues, clients and friends to create Windmills: a social-value organisation that aims to help people be all they can be and make their difference in the world.

Since our inception, we have helped over 30,000 individuals – from 5–85 year olds, including young people, graduates, leaders, volunteers, parents, entrepreneurs, women returners, managers, trainees, as well as both unemployed and underemployed individuals – and even retirees (it's never too late to make a change). And still we aim to go on from strength to strength and spread the word that you can change your life. To this end, in 2011 we established the Windmills Foundation, a charity committed to inspiring young people to make the world a better place.

At Windmills we are passionate about helping people realise their full potential, and we practise what we preach. We've been through every single exercise in this book in our own personal pursuits to have No Regrets on Sunday – and we know they will equip you with all you need to change your life.

introduction

Each and every one of us is a special individual with a unique combination of skills, talents, experiences, passions and motivations in life – and you have choices as to how you are going to make the most of them. This book will not tell you what to do and how to live your life, but it will make you aware of the things you didn't realise you already knew and show you how you can use this knowledge to change your life for the better.

The ideas within these pages aim to provide you with a practical structure that will enable you to take a greater level of ownership and control over your life and to discover how to use the tools and techniques you need to sustain this over a lifetime. This book will not change your life – it's the person holding it that will. You!

HAVING THE TIME OF YOUR LIFE

At the last estimate there were about six billion of us on this planet; each and every one is a unique individual, and yet among this great number of people we find that we all only have two things in common: we are all born, and we will all die. The time in between these two events is our life and because we only get one shot at it, why not make it the best it can be?

Each of you will be at different stages and situations in your lives right now, and you will all have picked up this book for different reasons. You may be on a bit of a rollercoaster ride of change, uncertainty and transition, or you may be stuck in a rut, feeling unfulfilled or underemployed, drifting and looking for a new challenge or opportunity. Equally, you may just be feeling bumped or bruised by life's events and need a confidence boost or perhaps you simply want to get off the merry-go-round of life and gain a greater sense of control, purpose and meaning. Wherever you are in your journey through life, remember that you are not alone – there are literally millions of other people in the same position.

But before you get started on the seven-day programme outlined in this book, here are three simple questions you need to ask yourself:

1 Do you know the seven skills you love using and are good at?

2 Are you maximising these for a purpose or role you are passionate about?

3 Are you in a place and with the people who inspire and energise you each day?

We've asked these same questions to over 10,000 individuals – from graduates to grandparents, pupils to professionals, corporate employees to careers advisers. Amazingly, only 3 per cent of participants could answer yes to all three questions, which means that 97 per cent were not fully maximising their potential.

Can you answer YES to all three questions? Are you being the best you can be and truly having the time of your life? To answer this it's worth looking at what's happening right now in your life – your weekly routine.

NO REGRETS ON SUNDAY

Most of us crawl out of bed on Monday morning and drag ourselves through the week until we can heave a sigh of relief on Friday night. Then, on Saturday, we finally start to relax. On Sunday, there's hardly time to pause and think about our lives before the routine of another week kicks in. If we don't take time to think, some of us become trapped on that treadmill as week follows week, allowing the same old timetable, the same old habits and the same old moans to dictate our daily lifestyle. For others there may simply be an acceptance that their lives are satisfactory, if perhaps a little bland and lacking in challenge. For those people, too, it's sometimes easier to accept the routine as their lot in life.

Whatever stage of our life or career we are at, most of us are reluctant to ask ourselves why we are here, where we are going, who needs us most and how are we going to make the most of the time we have left. The big danger is that we end up waiting for that final 'weekend' when our working lives are over – the time when we retire and do all those things we've been promising ourselves we will do for years.

If this scenario sounds familiar, this book is for you. By simply setting aside an hour or so each day for the next week you can start to gain a fresh perspective on the way you think about and act on your life. Read on, and you will see how easy it is to make the changes that will stop you looking back when it's too late and regretting you didn't do something sooner. The only way to have no regrets when that distant Sunday comes is to start changing your life *now*.

IT'S TIME TO REFLECT

The key concept to making changes is to focus your mind on the job in hand. Try imagining your life as a single week, starting on Monday. With each day equal to around a dozen years, you're in your twenties by Tuesday, middle-aged by Thursday and heading for retirement on Friday night.

WHAT DAY OF THE WEEK ARE YOU ON?

It doesn't matter which day you are up to, what really counts is how you're going to make the most of the rest of your week.

MONDAY
AM = 0-6 years old/PM = 7-12 years old

TUESDAY
AM = 13-18 years old/PM = 19-24 years old

WEDNESDAY
AM = 25-30 years old/PM = 31-36 years old

THURSDAY
AM = 37-42 years old/PM = 43-48 years old

FRIDAY
AM = 49-54 years old/PM = 55-60 years old

SATURDAY
AM = 61-66 years old/PM = 67-72 years old

SUNDAY
AM = 73-78 years old/PM = 79-84 years old

BANK HOLIDAY
84+ years old

NO MAN IS AN ISLAND

As you progress through this book, remember to consider your relationships with other people as well as your own personal hopes and dreams.

Think about the people you love. Are they at the beginning, middle or end of their week? Does this have any implications for your life and how are you going to share what you have learned with them?

SEVEN DAYS TO CHANGE YOUR LIFE

If you don't take control of your life, who will? This book will provide you with a blueprint of steps you can take to make sure you have No Regrets on Sunday. So, over to you.

Spend seven days working through the following pages and you'll be amazed at how much you can achieve in just one week. From the minute you wake up on Monday morning to the moment you fall asleep on Sunday night, life presents you with seven days of possibilities. With possibility comes choice – choice over how you manage your lives.

No Regrets on Sunday will help you to pause and consider what's really important to you, to create wishes for the rest of the week and to take positive action today.

Each day you'll explore another positive step you can make. You'll learn to understand yourself better, to change how you look at the world, and to discover how you can use your time more creatively to get what you really need. Committing time to the daily exercises in this book will show you how all the different aspects of your life – working, learning, playing and giving – can help you meet that challenge. And by the end of the seven days you should be able to picture the kind of life you wish to lead and will know how to acquire the skills and support you require in order to realise your ambitions and enjoy your life to the full.

Here's a snapshot of each step in the week ahead, and how we will guide you to achieve your ultimate goal of No Regrets on Sunday:

MONDAY: MINDSET

Can you change a habit of a lifetime? To make the right changes you may need to review how you think about your life.

TUESDAY: TIME

How can you make the most of the time you have? The solution lies in finding more creative ways of blending the four key areas of your life: working, learning, playing and giving.

WEDNESDAY: WHO

At the end of the day, who are you and who do you really want to be? The answer lies in the roles you play today and in being honest with yourself about what are the most important roles for the future.

THURSDAY: TALENTS

What are the talents and skills you love using most and how can you maximise them? You have a unique combination of skills you love using and are really good at. What opportunities are available today for you to use them?

FRIDAY: FULFILMENT

Is your life simply full or truly fulfilling? True fulfilment comes when you combine your passions with purposes or causes that are meaningful to your lives or those of others.

SATURDAY: SATISFACTION

How can you make all your hopes, dreams and aspirations a reality? By creating your Golden Ticket (see page 131), an inspiring vision for your future life to come.

SUNDAY: SUPPORT

What support do you need to sustain yourself? The support of your friends, family and mentors is vital throughout this week.

MAKING THE MOST OF THIS BOOK

The ideas in this book will help you to make decisions that will change your life. However, to make that happen you need to give yourself time to concentrate on what is being asked of you. The chapters are designed to take up only an hour of your time each day, but if you need longer, do each section at a pace that suits you. Try to ensure that you find some quiet time every day to work on the book – perhaps an hour at the beginning of the day, and take some time at the end of the day to think through each chapter again and to review how the task has gone.

You may find that certain chapters will resonate more deeply and appear more relevant to you and your life. If this is the case, don't deprive yourself of any extra time that you need to take – either at that point or at the end of the week. And don't start during a week when you have lots of other pressures and dead-lines – give yourself the opportunity to really make this the major focus of your week.

Record your thoughts and ideas as you go through the book and you can review them later and see how far you have travelled and how your ideas have changed. You might find that it helps to share the process with someone else who can encourage you during your week – as you can them.

Celebrate your progress as you go along and again at the end of the week. Remember, with every step you take you are already on the way to ensuring you have No Regrets on Sunday.

Lastly, and most importantly, have confidence in your ability. Don't let doubt hold you back; take that first determined step and keep moving forward, day by day.

READ, THINK, ACT

The ideas in this book are based on encouraging you to think and act differently. So, the week ahead will see each day divided into three sections that will help you achieve the goal of the day:

READ: Helps you to be aware of the topical theme for the day.

THINK: Enables you to gain a deeper insight and understanding of what this means to you.

ACT: Encourages you to complete a 'task for today' and commit to one simple brave step to move forward.

CHANGING THE WAY YOU LIVE YOUR LIFE

Please don't fall into the trap of merely reading this book and thinking you've done it all. The premise of *No Regrets on Sunday* is taking action, however big or small, so please make sure you try out all the exercises and tasks outlined on each day. If you find you are struggling to do them by yourself, find someone who will go through them with you, or employ a 'chief motivator' to spur you on.

There are case studies throughout this book to inspire you and help keep your ideas on track. They all come from people who have read this book, have been on one of our programmes here at Windmills, have spent time with us or have just been keen to share their story with you.

Of course, you can't just get through the week and expect everything to automatically be different for the rest of your life. In order to have No Regrets on Sunday you need to incorporate the new vision and approach to your life.

This process does not finish at the end of this week; it needs to be something that becomes a lifetime habit. So to help you we have included an additional chapter – No Regrets for Life – which will provide advice on how to make No Regrets on Sunday a part of your life and keep the positive focus and ideas you have worked hard all week to achieve.

If you need proof that this programme works, there are case-studies throughout the book from many other people who have engaged in the no regrets process as well as 101 examples of simple actions participants have taken to continue the process started by this week on pages 201–210.

So read on, what have you got to lose? By dedicating just one hour a day to reading this book and exploring your life you can find a way to change your future and enable you to have No Regrets on Sunday.

1

MONDAY
MINDSET

Life is 5% about what happens
to us and 95% how we
respond to what happens to us

'What would you attempt to do
if you knew you could not fail?'

Unknown

READ...

STOP THE SLEEPWALKING

The moment we wake up on Monday morning we almost start sleepwalking through our daily life. Automatically, we switch into a series of habitual routines; we get out of the same side of the bed, brush our teeth using the same hand and turn on the taps in the same way.

Once downstairs, we might head to the kitchen and set about a prescribed routine of opening cupboards, switching on appliances and making breakfast. Our daily activities often then follow the same familiar pattern – locking the front door, setting the alarm, getting into the car, train or bus and travelling down the same streets, and meeting and greeting the same people as we tread a well-worn path to our daily destination.

It's not just the habits in that first hour of the day that follow a set pattern: most of us also have systems for working, shopping, talking with our partners and even doing the washing and ironing. Virtually everything we do on a daily basis involves a series of learned habits.

In fact, we act rather like robots programmed by a number of pre-set default switches. These switches not only affect the choice of our activities, but also dictate our thoughts and feelings, which in turn affect our behaviour. These thoughts and feelings govern our view of the day ahead – whether we see it as an exciting possibility or just another manic Monday. They influence our views about work, too, and whether we consider it a prison sentence or a fun day out. They also determine how we respond to change – whether we resist it as a threat or welcome it as an opportunity.

Today you're embarking on the first of seven days that could change your life. Just spend an hour each day taking in the ideas put forward in these chapters and you'll find yourself thinking differently by Sunday. You'll feel more satisfied as you look back on your week, and as you act on those ideas you'll be on track to spend every day in a new way that will save you a lifetime of regrets.

'It is not the mountain we conquer but ourselves.'

Edmund Hillary

SWITCH TO A NEW MINDSET

In order to make a change that lasts, the crucial thing you must understand is that *you* control those switches – the way you set those defaults sets your mindset. If you're not quite sure what your mindset is at the moment, and therefore how you need to change it to make a difference in your life, ask yourself what your default settings might be in the following situations:

- In a traffic jam, a car is trying to sneak in front of you from a side road – do you let them in or drive on?

- You come home after a hard day's work and your partner is lying on the couch with the house in a mess – do you start an argument or tidy up?

- You are forced to go out with a couple from hell – do you spend the evening sulking or try to have a good time regardless?

- Your boss postpones a scheduled meeting you've been preparing for – do you fume and let frustration get the better of you, or do you use that time productively instead and rearrange the appointment?

You should find you can immediately answer these questions without much hesitation. Your response is your default setting, which can easily trigger a train of thought in your head, although this isn't always helpful in your quest to take on a new mindset.

For example, you meet an old boyfriend – or girlfriend – holding hands with a new partner. Do you congratulate or ignore them? If you ignore them, do you start thinking, 'Why are they so close? Were they seeing one another when we were together? Did they have an affair while I was on the scene?' Or perhaps there is rumour of redundancy going round the office. Before you know it you think you are the one who has been targeted, and then believe you've lost your job and will never get another. This thought process then leads on to you imagining losing the house and experiencing a family break-up as a result. And by the way, this thought process had started as a rumour of redundancy rather than a real fact.

As each new idea crowds in, your train of thought starts to veer off track. Worry simply means you are using your imagination in the wrong way.

Clearly, it's not life's events but the way you respond to them that shapes your future. The problem is that, just like breathing, you do so many things without even thinking about them – subconsciously deciding to be happy or sad, relaxed or stressed, positive or negative. These habits are ingrained in you through your parents' influence, the environment you grew up in, your peers, society at large, and even the media.

Sadly, such habits often stop you from developing and living the kind of lives you really want; and when they have governed you for so long, they can be hard to shake off.

The key to changing the habits of a lifetime is to be aware of them in the first place. The best way to cope with the uncertainties of the week ahead and have No Regrets on Sunday is to shift your mindset by changing some of those default settings that control your habits.

So, as you travel to work, do your shopping or surf the internet, start questioning those actions that you do automatically. What old habits do you need to discard? What part of your life could benefit from a fresh approach? What new habits would it be helpful for you to develop today? Try thinking differently about 'self-limiting beliefs'; stop thinking of yourself negatively and stop making excuses such as 'I haven't got the time or money'. Start thinking positively – today.

THINK...

WHAT'S ON YOUR PLATE?

From birth to death, life dishes up some landmark events. But along the way we find many other things on our plate too. We are all born, and through the course of our lives we learn about our values, the importance of health and love and the different roles that we will play over our lifetimes. Change affects us all. Sometimes we are broken and down, at other times we feel content and happy. There are exciting surprises and all sorts of different possibilities in store for us, but at the end of the day we are all here for a purpose.

Have you ever been asked 'What have you got on your plate today?' as you step out of the door in the morning? In reality it is probably not just one thing but a whole host of issues. Have you ever heard people saying they are trying to keep a number of plates spinning at any one time?

Imagine you had an empty dinner plate in front of you – what would be on your plate today?

Here are some of the things that people on our Windmills programmes have had dished up to them. Pick the ones that you feel are current for you now:

Surprises

Children

Security

Love

Battles

Health

Relationships

Challenge

Redundancy

Sadness

Pressure

Freedom

Success

Passions

Barriers

Change

Variety

Roles

Crisis

Celebrations

Work

Family

Values

Happiness

Death

Travel

Learning

Opportunities

Wealth

Purpose

Separation

Debt

Competition

Chance

Faith

Uncertainty

Employability

Lifestyle

Potential

Job

Career

Birth

Well-being

Worry

Rejection

Frustration

Volunteering

Ambition

Hope

Balance

Friendship

Now imagine you are sitting around a table with friends celebrating the most amazing year of your life. Over the past year you have got everything you want on your plate – so from the list above, or your own list, what's on it now?

EAT = EVENT, ACTION, THINKING

The positive thing to remember is that it's not the event (E) that determines the outcome, it is two other factors – the way that you respond or act (A) and this in turn is affected by how you think (T) about the situation. This is never more apparent than when you see the stories of people who cope amazingly with disaster, disability or death, while at the same time others seem to be enjoying an easier lifestyle but in fact are looking enviously at what's on someone else's plate. In a business situation, there are also people who take their work for granted. It is only when the work part of their 'plate' is taken away from them that they realise how important things such as social contact with their colleagues, and a sense of purpose and structure to the day, is to them.

So ask yourself the question, 'How do I have to act and think differently to create an inspiring future for myself? How do I need to change my EATing habits?' The exciting thing is that you have far more control over your life than you can ever imagine. Allow yourself to act and think in a different way and remember that you may need to break things down into small bite-sized chunks, just like you did when learning to EAT as a child.

> 'Do not follow where the path may lead. Go instead where there is no path and leave a trail.'
>
> **Muriel Strode**

■ CASE STUDY: Don't judge a book by its cover

At the age of 20, Simon was still immersed in the first challenging chapter of his life. Leaving school early, with no qualifications and very little sense of control, his only income and feelings of self-worth came from helping his uncle carry kitchen units for a couple of hours a week. It was during a kitchen fitting that he saw a copy of *No Regrets on Sunday* on the couch. He thought nothing of it and got into his uncle's car at the end of the job, but something had been triggered in his mind and so he raced back into the house and asked to borrow the book.

Several weeks later, Simon had finished the book and now realised he had to change the plot of his life story and create his first break. He had always had an interest in cars, so he decided to take the test to qualify as a taxi driver. A job like this was not reliant on formal qualifications, would give Simon the freedom to spend time with his family and also bring in a decent income. All he needed to do was to pass 'the Knowledge' test (knowing the best routes to destinations), but he was so desperate to start the new chapter of his life that he cheated by bringing in a road map – and was caught out by the examiner.

Up until this point in his life, Simon's instinctive response to a challenge from authority was to use his fists or mouth aggressively. However, it was at this tipping point that he remembered reading this mindset section of *No Regrets on Sunday* and consciously decided to change a habit of a lifetime. With a deep breath, he apologised and explained honestly how much he wanted this opportunity and that he would do anything to secure it. To his great surprise, the examiner let him take the test again. He passed it with flying colours and the rest is history.

Later, Simon's uncle returned the book to its owner, informing them that his nephew was now financially independent and felt worth something for the first time, and that the book had turned his whole life around. But it wasn't the book that had done that – by making a decision to change his mindset, in an instant Simon had changed his life forever!

YOUR PERSONAL EATING HABITS

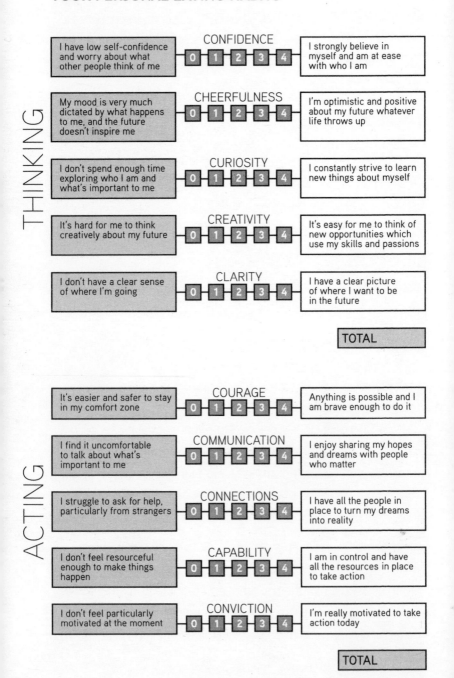

Opposite are 10 EATing habits which will help you achieve your goal of having no regrets in life. For each habit, circle the number that best represents where you think you lie between the two statements. Be totally honest in your answers – there are no rights or wrongs, nor anybody to impress.

You'll notice that the first five habits are asking you about the way you think, and the second five about the way you act.

Add together your first five scores, then add together your second five. You'll now have a combined score for 'thinking' and a combined score for 'acting'. Use these scores as a grid reference to plot your position on the graph below. Work out which box you fall into, then read the information and case studies below to find out what you must do to move your life forward.

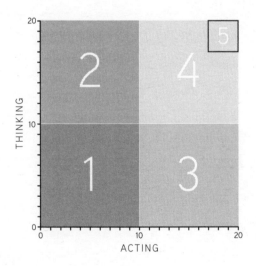

BOX 1: YES BUT ...

Do you find yourself making 'reasonable excuses' about why things aren't working out? 'Yes Buts' often focus on the problems rather than possibilities, blame others rather than themselves, and react to what life dishes up rather than take control of it. Remember, if you're not part of the solution, you're part of the problem!

Consider how your life will end up if you carry on week in week out in the same way. Will you have any regrets? Remember, you have far more potential than you could ever imagine.

■ CASE STUDY: Small steps to make a change

Susan was fearful of what some of the changes she felt were facing her would mean. She knew things needed to change – and there were a lot of them: her job, her relationships, her personal approach and thinking – but she continued to do nothing about them other than complain to those around her.

She believed that as bad as it may be where she was, it had to be better than 'opening the box and not being able to put the lid back on'. She worried that she wouldn't know what she was starting, and wouldn't be able to finish or stop it.

So in this situation, Susan needed to consider whether her approach was really helping her to think and act differently. While she may have had lots of things she needed to tackle, it is the combination of small steps and little things that build up to make the bigger differences, and this was the best starting point for her to make changes to her life.

Like Susan, you may need to pick one smaller thing – something that you feel you stand a chance of tackling successfully – and work on that first. Get someone to support you in doing this and use this to build confidence to take on some of the larger things facing you. Be honest with yourself, though – you have got to want to do it, and some people in this box get used to repeating the same negative message of 'I am a victim and life never goes well for me'. This kind of personal approach and behaviour can often keep these people exactly where they are in life, with no prospect of moving on.

BOX 2: IF ONLY …

Are you a bit of a dreamer? Do you have lots of great ideas but rarely follow through and turn them into reality? Does 'I'll do it someday, sometime!' sound like something you'd say? 'If Onlys' are forever putting things off: if only I'd been braver, if only I'd asked for help, if only I'd talked to someone about it; if only I'd stuck with it … Think of all the regrets you may have if you don't have the courage of your own convictions. If *you* don't do it, who will?

■ CASE STUDY: Don't delay – act now

Tony had always dreamed of running his own show and being his own boss and he had worked hard to become the owner of a small IT business. While doing this he was the compulsive 'hobby enthusiast' and threw himself into a range of other interests with his usual passion and energy outside of work whenever he could. He began to recognise that the day job was a lot less satisfying than the things he was doing away from work.

Tony began to give this some thought, and as he did so he became aware that one of these hobbies was becoming much more than that. As he trained to be a 'first responder' Tony realised he had a real passion and desire to become a paramedic. However, he believed he couldn't do this – how could he build financial security in his business while at the same time retraining for another unrelated career? His approach to making things happen was not helping and although he was being really active in some respects, he was in fact failing to act on the one thing that would make a significant difference to his life – his work!

He discussed his dilemma with a friend who was also about to start their own business, who advised him 'don't just think about it, do it'.

BOX 3: NO IDEA

Do you ever find yourself busily rushing through life like a headless chicken? Lots of action, lots of talking, lots of energy, but no real focus or direction. 'No Ideas' are great at acting; they'll jump into anything head first, but they're not so good at thinking: where's this taking me? Does it creatively combine my skills, passions and values? Does it make me happy? The danger is that if you don't stop and think about your life you may spend the rest of your years going round in circles, then later on have regrets that you missed out on something really important.

■ CASE STUDY: Stop, think, and move on

For Steve, a new promotion offered a great opportunity to expand his skills and take on new challenges. Once he had taken on the role, very quickly his responsibilities grew and the support he had initially received was taken away.

Steve still felt passionately about what he did but he was getting swamped by the volume of work he was doing. He began to feel that he was busier 'acting' than ever before – running around doing lots but failing to see if any of it was taking him in the direction he wanted to go in. Added to which he believed this weight of work was damaging his passion and enthusiasm for his job, because it reduced his personal energy levels, leaving him shattered at the end of every day.

What Steve needed to do was the simplest, and also the hardest, thing for him – to STOP. To make a difference in his life and to regain his passion for his job, he needed to stop rushing round and reflect on where he was at the time, where he wanted to be and how he could move himself there.

BOX 4: ACTION THINKER

Are you someone who has learned to take control by thinking and acting differently, or does it come naturally? 'Action Thinkers' are a bit like helicopters – they have the confidence and ability to rise up and see the bigger picture, but they also have the responsiveness to position themselves so that they can seize opportunities as they appear.

Some words of caution from our years of experience are, 'are you really fit enough to fly?' Be honest with yourself and make sure you've been totally accurate with your scores and have the evidence to back them up. Don't try to impress others or feel you have to be seen to be doing well: the danger is that you may well crash and burn on the long haul!

After this long safety warning – congratulations, you're well on your way.

■ **CASE STUDY: Don't give up the things you love**

For Jayne, major changes were on the horizon. After over thirty years within a profession she loved the time had come to retire. A whole new chapter in her life was about to open up.

Understandably, a step like this was exciting, but she also felt some trepidation. She had thought about all the things that her current role did not allow her time to do – those hobbies, skills and passions that had to be shoe-horned into her working life over the last thirty years. She explored options to learn more about them, find groups that used them and worked with her husband to explore how together they could pursue these in retirement.

Jayne knew that she would really miss the young people she had worked with over her thirty-year career, and so she considered how she could support this age group going forward. Although initially tentative, Jayne started to explore options to do this and spoke with her network of friends and colleagues to develop possibilities for when she felt the time would be right.

By making sure that her thinking and acting were working in tandem, Jayne created a plan for a fulfilling and purposeful retirement built on the things she loved.

BOX 5: NO REGRETS

If you passed away today, would you have absolutely no regrets? 'No Regrets' are outstanding thinkers and actors; they are at ease with who they are and clear about where they want to be, but they also treat every day as though it was their last. Just as importantly, they have the courage, connections, creativity, capability and convictions to make their hopes and dreams a reality. No Regrets believe in the art of the possible and are not held back by their own or other people's baggage. As with Action Thinkers, No Regrets must be able to walk the talk and provide practical evidence in their daily lives.

It's all well and good to read and think about doing something fresh and new, but is it motivating and purposeful enough for you to really act on it? And even then, are you going to take that brave step to act and make it real? 'Some day' is not a day of the week. If you don't take responsibility for your mindset and your own direction in life, who will?

■ CASE STUDY: Making sense of life

As we journey through the ups and downs, twists and turns of life, we all need a pit stop to refuel, refresh and make sense of where we're going.

Whenever I feel a bit low or in need of inspiration, I'm privileged to be able to stop off at an oasis in the desert – a special needs primary school where I can go and leave my ego in the locker outside. We all have an ego to some degree and how you control it depends on your mindset; the ego is that self-centred character that worries about the past or strives for the future without enjoying the present.

So, at this school one day, in the hydrotherapy pool, I met Jan and her husband with their son, Matthew. Matthew was once a fit and healthy 10-year-old, but you never know what's around the corner. The family lived by a busy road and Matthew loved playing football. However, despite many warnings from his parents, one awful day he chased a ball out into the road and ran straight into the path of an oncoming car.

The accident left Matthew paralysed from the neck down; he has lost his ability to communicate verbally and he now requires help with his eating, drinking and toileting. The lives of Matthew and his parents have been turned upside down, but, amazingly, when I met them that day Jan and Dave were already beginning to come to terms with the situation. After the initial shock, denial, anger and frustration in the aftermath of the accident, and with the help of an amazing team of professionals, including teachers, support assistants, physios, health-care specialists and communications technology experts, Matthew's parents are coping remarkably well.

What really struck Jan was how much she had taken for granted before the accident and how even the smallest steps in Matthew's painfully slow development are appreciated and celebrated. She is now mindful of every tiny aspect of his growing up, any simple eye communication, finger movement, grunts and facial responses to stimulation.

What Jan wasn't prepared for and was nervous about was how she would react when she returned to work after 12 months' leave of absence. Her biggest worry was not how to cope with the new demands of her son, but how to manage the small-mindedness of some of her colleagues in the staff room, and having to listen to them moan about the same petty issues as they were a year ago, and the year before that, and the year before that …

Jan wanted to share her story in this book and to pass on her message to everyone: 'Stop worrying about the past or living in fear of the future. Enjoy the present because you literally don't know what's around the corner.'

'The only difference between a good day and a bad day is your attitude.'

Dennis S. Brown

If you are the person in the staff room Jan talked about, put your ego back in the locker and throw away the key!

ACT...

CREATE A NEW HABIT TODAY

So what single, small step can you take today to take control and ensure you have No Regrets on Sunday?

While you may not be able to control all the events that life dishes up for us, you can control the way you think about them and act on them or react to them. Having no regrets is about making choices that are right for you. How would you like to end your life – happy or sad? Bitter or sweet? Full-up or fed-up? How are you going to change the way you EAT today? What one new habit can you adopt now?

To create a new habit, you'll probably need to break an old one first. Put your energy into those things that are in your control to change rather than dwelling on those things that are either out of your control or are not actually true. Stop worrying and start living today. Look at the diagram below and you'll see that 92 per cent of our most common worries are absolutely needless.

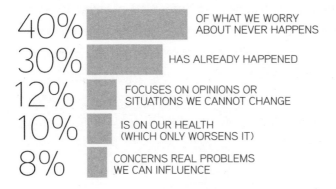

40% OF WHAT WE WORRY ABOUT NEVER HAPPENS

30% HAS ALREADY HAPPENED

12% FOCUSES ON OPINIONS OR SITUATIONS WE CANNOT CHANGE

10% IS ON OUR HEALTH (WHICH ONLY WORSENS IT)

8% CONCERNS REAL PROBLEMS WE CAN INFLUENCE

In order to make a change today, start by choosing the PERSONAL EATING habit (see page 10) that is easiest to work on and can make the greatest difference. Give yourself the aim to do something practical and simple today to improve this habit. Remember, it's easier to act your way into a new way of thinking than to think your way into a new way of acting.

Look back at your thinking/acting chart and use the advice below to help you to work with your strengths and weaknesses to make an effective change today.

BOX 1: YES BUT ...

Select that EATing habit that you would like to develop and improve, and think of three small steps that you can make yourself in the next 24 hours to change the situation. Now pick the action that causes you the least concern and make it happen. Once you have take this small step, give yourself a pat on the back. Perhaps you could think about taking one or both of the other steps today or in the upcoming week too. It's easy to look at the difficulties and pitfalls surrounding making changes, but once you start it becomes so much easier and you'll find a vastly increased self-belief that will make you want to carry on.

BOX 2: IF ONLY ...

Focus your energy on acting in a different way today. Select the EATing habit that you want to work on and be determined that you will make a small change. What calculated risk can you take? Who could you share your ideas with? Who could you ask for help? How could you start to take control and keep the momentum going? You don't have to look far into the future or over-analyse what you intend to do – ACT NOW and see where it takes you.

BOX 3: NO IDEA

First of all – be still, calm and breathe ... Today is about you and making a change for yourself. Make sure that you schedule in some 'me time' today. Spend time on the things that are important to you rather than the many tasks given to you as urgent. Check your whole attitude and approach to the day ahead – how can you think differently about yourself and your future today? And then take steps to change that EATing habit that you know you can make a difference to and improve your entire life.

BOX 4: ACTION THINKER/BOX 5: NO REGRETS

Remember, in order to have absolutely no regrets you may need to set your sights even higher or practise even more so that you can respond to future winds of change. We all have the potential to be happy, and to have no regrets, so look at what you can do today to bring meaning and life to those two words.

Try to find some time at the end of the day or after your action has been completed to process what you have achieved. Take out a notebook and briefly answer the following questions:

- WHAT DID YOU HOPE TO ACHIEVE BY YOUR ACTION?

- WHAT WAS YOUR BIGGEST FEAR/CONCERN ABOUT MAKING THIS STEP AND DID IT COME TRUE?

- HOW DO YOU FEEL NOW THAT YOU HAVE COMPLETED THE TASK?

- THINK OF THREE POSITIVE OUTCOMES FROM MAKING THIS CHANGE – these can be for you or for others, and can be directly related to your action or to your state of mind.

■ CASE STUDY: Who needs eyesight when you have vision?

Colin is an amazing young man and is quite simply one of the inspirations for this book. I first met him, aged 17 years old, and his guide dog, Lyka, waiting at a bus stop.

My eyesight is terrible, but I managed to see what I thought was a bus in the distance. I asked Colin whether this was his bus, to which he replied 'No'. So I asked, 'How do you know?' and he said, 'It doesn't have the sound of my bus's engine.' Amazingly, Colin has developed other listening skills to compensate for his visual impairment. We got talking and I found out that he was preparing to run in the Paralympics, but unfortunately he didn't have enough guide runners to support him. Before I knew it I'd volunteered to help out and the next week we met up and went for a jog. It was like the blind leading the blind and was a pretty hairy experience for both of us, considering the pot holes on the Liverpool streets and the fact that Colin was faster than me and sometimes leading the way!

Over the next six months I was blown away by Colin's attitude, belief in himself and his foresight in how he would conduct his life. He had already achieved one of his goals – to play oboe in the youth orchestra. For each performance he had the imagination and creativity to first buy the CD of the concert, then ask his tutor to play and record the oboe part. He would then listen and learn these pieces off by heart.

Colin never saw his disability as a barrier to anything that he wanted to achieve, and went on to play the drums in a band as well as run for his country. He has achieved more by Tuesday afternoon in the week of his life than many of us hope for in our lifetime!

Colin has continued to embrace the ideas in no regrets by embarking on a new chapter of his life and enrolling on a music degree. He has had to stretch his comfort zone again by travelling on two buses to college. For those of you who, like many I've told this story to, say 'What happens if a different bus turns up?' Colin's reply is simple: 'What's the point of worrying about something that may never happen? And if it does, there's probably some mad person at the bus stop who will help me out!'

You may have perfect eyesight, but are you blind to the enormous potential and possibilities you have in life? Do you see barriers that aren't even there?

BE MINDFUL

If you want to think and act in a different way, you first need to be more mindful of how you currently think and act. How conscious are you of what you are doing?

Begin by asking yourself: are you being the best you can be here and now? Do you find your mind wandering to something that happened earlier, thinking about what you are doing later, or just generally being distracted by the normal 'chatter of life'? If so, try to look around you and notice the things that you take for granted as you busily rush through life – your health, family, friends, the opportunities that you are presented with and the natural environment. Open your eyes to all that is around you and how you respond to it, and try to be more aware.

So as Monday draws to a close, you've started on the road to change. You've worked on mindset, so tomorrow you are ready to look at how you spend your time, as you explore Tuesday's task. Before you move on, though, take a moment to think about the key ideas we've discussed here for changing your mindset.

MONDAY: RECAP

- *Determine what your mindset is now and what you'd like it to be.*

- *Be grateful and appreciative for what you have got and can achieve and use this to help minimise the worry and anxiety about what you cannot change.*

- *Decide which habits you'd like to lose, and which you'd like to adopt – ask yourself how you can change your EATing habits for good.*

'Keep your mind open to change at all times. Welcome it. Court it. It is only by examining and re-examining your opinions and ideas that you can progress.'

Dale Carnegie

2

TUESDAY
TIME

You probably spend more
time planning your two-week
holiday than the other 50 weeks
of the year

'A man who dares to waste one hour
of life has not discovered the value of life.'

Charles Darwin

READ...

MAKE THE MOST OF THE TIME GIVEN TO YOU

As you journey through an average week you have all sorts of calls on your time. You face the need to earn a living, care for others, stay fit, keep the house tidy, enjoy hobbies, and also to socialise. But all the time you are being presented with choices; you can choose which of these activities to build into each day, decide whether or not to do them separately or together, then think about how you view them. You may have to do these things – but do you view them as fun or as a chore?

Now think hard about what's in your diary for the rest of this week. You'll quickly realise it is made up of different combinations of the following four types of activity: working, learning, playing and giving (WLPG):

WORKING

This applies to any form of paid or unpaid career, part- or full-time employment, or self-employment.

LEARNING

It may be both formal and informal, on the job, or done through experience, courses or old-fashioned trial and error.

PLAYING

This includes the things you do to enjoy yourself inside or outside work and enjoying time with your family and friends, and it is not solely confined to weekends and time off.

GIVING

It does not simply mean donating money, but giving your time, energy, talents and skills to purposes and people who need support, to your family, friends and colleagues as part of your everyday life.

The first step is to recognise each and every one of these elements and apply them to your own situation. Once you have done this, you can make each day more enjoyable and worthwhile by blending these four key areas of activity. It is the quality and blend of your working, learning, playing and giving (WLPG) that shapes your life.

If you keep these ideas in your mind all week, you'll be thinking and feeling differently by Sunday – and you'll be well on the way to ensuring you have no regrets.

■ CASE STUDY: Are you an elephant or a flea?

The Elephant is the slow-moving beast of an organisation that plods on for years and finds it hard to quickly change direction; the Flea is the fast-moving, flexible and agile entrepreneurial creature that is happiest when it is free to flit about with its own spirit in its own space.

Charlene was mid-career and working in Human Resources. She described herself as a corporate car park attendant, moving executive resources from one level to another. She had lost the 'human' bit of human resources and had become frustrated, disillusioned and no longer able to use her initiative.

She came to us at Windmills for help, and we discussed with her the story of the cumbersome Elephant and the Flea. Charlene realised that she was more like a Flea, but that for the past 20 years she had fed off the dung of the Elephant and was in danger of being swallowed up and becoming an Elephant herself.

She met another like-minded Flea, Rob, and they married soon after. Together they worked to create a portfolio career that combined Charlene's interest in writing on business issues with her partner's passion for photography. For half the year they live in London, where Charlene takes on the role of the main breadwinner and her husband acts as the home keeper. For the other half they retire to a small cottage on the coast; there their roles reverse and the photography business becomes the main work focus and Charlene reverts to a supportive home-keeping role.

More recently both Charlene and Rob have combined their writing skills with photography to produce a highly visual book which tells the positive stories of people's lives. Interestingly, both their children have modelled their lives on their parents, working from home in a Flea-like manner.

Charlene is very aware that Elephants and Fleas both need each other. Fleas need to feed off the Elephant (gaining the things that a large organisation can provide), and Elephants need the agility of Fleas (to inject new ideas and spread innovation).

So, are you an Elephant or a Flea?

Two words of warning before you decide. If you are an elephant grazing happily in the comfort zone and relative safety of your large organisation, watch out for the corporate hunters – they can shoot at will, ready to eliminate targets to achieve their aims.

If you are a Flea, try to avoid banging your head against the glass ceiling. You have tremendous potential; be creative, and realise that potential by finding new heights to aim for.

LEARN TO BLEND YOUR WLPG

The problem is that we usually see working, learning, playing and giving as distinct areas with few links between them. In the past, it was common for people to see their whole lifespan as boxed off into four totally different sections. The traditional pattern dictated years at school, followed by a lifetime of work, ending with a spell of retirement that involved the two elements of playing and giving.

Today, however, many people try to achieve a balance between these WLPG areas – dividing their time between working, learning, playing and giving. In theory, if a person divided their time between these four areas equally, you could show it as it appears in Diagram 1. The four areas here are shown to be equal in size and there is no overlap between them – each is simply balanced against the other.

In reality, though, when in employment, work dominates most people's lives (see Diagram 2), which is why the WLPG pattern of a person in this situation shows W as the largest area. This person is juggling the four areas, but none of them overlap.

Balancing WLPG is a compromise – more time for one area means less for another. This can soon lead to an imbalance. In fact, this example is a powerful symbol of modern life, where some people are in danger of becoming wage-slaves (with little or no LPG), just to keep up the lifestyle (the P) they have become accustomed to. The irony is that in our quest for the next 'must have', work monopolises our lives, leaving little time to enjoy the things we've worked so hard to pay for!

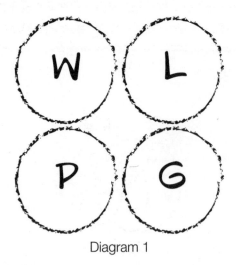

Diagram 1

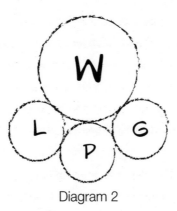

Diagram 2

But there is another approach we can all take to our daily working, learning, playing and giving. Rather than simply balancing these four areas, we can look for opportunities through which we can combine or blend them. Blending just two of these four areas can really enrich the quality of your life. The more of these areas you can blend – two, three, or even all four – throughout your life, the greater your chance of becoming more fulfilled, employable and happy.

The WLPG diagram below (Diagram 3) shows some overlap between working and learning, with playing and giving linking in to both. It suggests that this person's work provides some learning opportunities and that both the work and the learning are a source of enjoyment.

Diagram 3

Remember, we are all unique – there is no set formula that works for everyone. Some people work to live; others live to work. For some, work is all about learning, playing and giving; others may not have a work circle at all. Other people may see play as something they do only with friends outside of work. Inevitably, over time as you go on your journey through life, the balance and blend of these four areas will change. However, it is a well-known fact that you contribute most when you're having fun, learning and stretching yourselves and using the skills you love and are good at.

'It all depends on how we look at things, and not on how they are themselves.'

Carl Jung

So, starting today, Tuesday, how are you going to allocate the rest of your week in terms of working, learning, playing and giving? How will these four areas overlap? The sketches opposite provide a few classic examples, but the choice is uniquely yours.

To help maximise the blend you create, consider:

- Being open to possibilities. Rather than seeing working, learning, playing and giving as occupying various time frames, approach them as four different aspects of the same time frame.

- Being creative and remember to encircle your day the right way. For example, you could approach today as being full of fun (with P enclosing W, L and G), or as a day of giving (with G enclosing W, L and P).

- Making a conscious choice of how you hope to embrace the day ahead; you will dramatically change its outcome.

LIVING HAPPY
A sense of fun embraces the whole day.

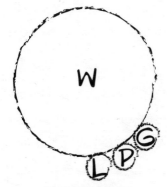

BURNED OUT
Unfulfilling work gobbles up life.

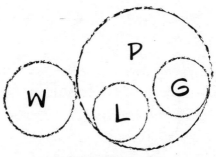

WORKING TO LIVE
Earning money to fuel a passion.

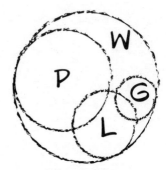

WORKAHOLIC
Passionate about work but no rest and play.

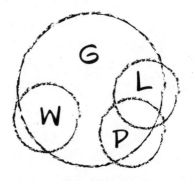

GENEROUS
Making a difference is more important.

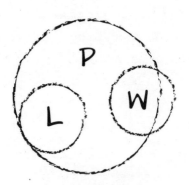

SELF-CENTRED
All about me, no giving to others.

■ CASE STUDY: Playing the game of your life

Imagine your life as a game of football, with each of the 90 minutes of the game being one year of your life.

Max was fast approaching half-time in his forties. He had been battered and bruised by a range of challenging tackles, from racism and prejudices, as well as facing opposition from unemployment and underemployment. He had worked his way up the career pitch towards the goalposts and had become marketing director for a family owned gambling business. All good, but then his corporate team was bought out by a new owner with a radically new set of values and ambitions. Max saw the team morale dip dramatically. It was at this point in his life that Max came to us at Windmills and we helped coach him to reflect on the highlights of his first-half performance, focusing on his skills, passions, values and purpose in life.

'This time, like all times, is a very good one, if we but know what to do with it.'

Ralph Waldo Emerson

The interesting thing about a game of football is that after the half-time team talk the players go back on to the pitch and move forward in a new direction, trying to score in the opposite goal. The same thing had happened in Max's life after talking with us – by drawing his four circles, he realised his work was both unfulfilling, under-utilising his strengths, and unsatisfactory for his biggest supporters – his family.

Max wanted to blend his working, learning, playing and giving in a different way. His first step was to take some quality time out to reposition his WLPG circles and to then create a new and inspiring work role. So he set up a coffee bar, which coupled his entrepreneurial skills with a passion to lead a small creative team in the hospitality industry. With the support of his wife and new business partner, who complemented his various skills, Max has created a chain of coffee bars as well as a catering business.

Most importantly, in his mid-life team talk Max highlighted the importance of both family and community spirit and he now takes every Friday off so that he can have an extended weekend in which he can spend quality time with his three young children. Max's goals have changed, and he has freed himself up from the business to volunteer as a mentor for fledgling businesses and organises a range of fundraising events for British Red Cross.

Max's main message is, 'If you are unhappy with how the game of your life is going, there is no use being a spectator and moaning from the sidelines. You have to get on to the pitch and focus on the goals that really matter.'

THINK...

Assuming we will be lucky enough to live until our mid-eighties, we are born with 40 million minutes on the clock and counting. That's about 2.5 billion seconds!

The exciting thing is that we do have the time to achieve all we hope for in life. After all, each of us is given exactly the same number of hours, minutes and seconds each day. What counts is what we choose to do with them. Just imagine each second of your life as a tiny grain of sand slipping away through a giant egg timer. The real danger comes when we wish those millions of grains of sand away waiting for the weekend, the summer holiday, or even our retirement. We fail to use all that time in-between creatively and so we waste bucketfuls of sand along the way.

Of course we all have pressures on our time, but we also have far more control over it than we realise. For example, let's say you hoped to spend a third of your time working, a third travelling and having fun, and the final third learning a new language. This may sound hopeful, but you could easily go a step further. Instead of splitting your time three ways, how about blending the activities together? Perhaps you could spend half your time working and the other half travelling and learning a new language. Does that sound impossible? Not if you get creative and start thinking outside the box ... For instance, try finding a job you are passionate about which involves travelling around the world and provides the opportunity to learn a foreign language at the same time.

CREATING YOUR OWN BLEND

Today you could have around 1,000 minutes available to you – this next exercise will help you look at how you can creatively blend your working, learning, playing and giving to make the most of every single second of these minutes. Use your time creatively and you'll have No Regrets on Sunday.

STEP 1

Start by drawing your current blend of WLPG. Draw four circles, considering:

- THE SIZE OF EACH CIRCLE – this represents the time and energy you've put into working, learning, playing and giving over the past week. The more time you've spent on a particular area, the bigger that circle will be.

- THE OVERLAP BETWEEN CIRCLES – this highlights the level of overlap between WLP and G. For example, how much learning is going on in work, how much of work is fun and is a form of giving. In the example below, there's not much blending going on!

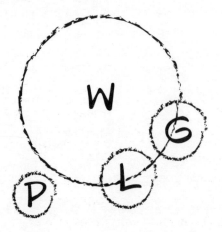

REFLECTION

ARE YOU HAPPY WITH YOUR WLPG CHART? What have you learned from this sketch? Does anything surprise or puzzle you?

DO YOU HAVE ANY OVERLAPS? What's happening, who are you with, where are you and what are you doing when two or more circles intersect?

WHAT KIND OF WLPG ARE YOU HAVING TODAY? Can you make any changes?

WHAT ARE THE IMPLICATIONS? What will happen, who will be affected if nothing changes?

Any WLPG sketch you draw is absolutely unique to you and simply reflects your current situation. The important thing to consider is how it will impact on you and other people if you allow it to stay the same for years to come. Whenever you have a pen in your hand, have a go at sketching out your current WLPG.

STEP 2

Now draw your ideal blend for the future: think of an appropriate time span, whether it is six months, a year or five years away, and fix a date in your mind. Now imagine yourself on that chosen day, having created your ideal WLPG blend. Sketch out that ideal, thinking creatively about the size of each circle and how they all overlap. Depending on your character and circumstance, you may wish to aim for your ideal or accept you have to compromise on certain aspects at particular stages in your life, e.g. giving is going to be big because I'm the main carer for an elderly relative, or perhaps I can't take that promotion just yet as it will mean a move of house and change of school for the children. Remember to be as creative as possible.

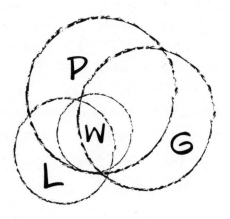

REFLECTION

WHAT EXCITES YOU MOST ABOUT WHAT YOU'VE DRAWN?

WHAT ARE THE MAJOR CHANGES YOU'VE MADE IN TERMS OF SIZE AND OVERLAP?

WHAT'S HAPPENING WHERE TWO OR MORE CIRCLES ARE BLENDED?

WHICH CIRCLE DID YOU DRAW FIRST? You may want to try this exercise again starting with the circle that is most important to you.

With a clear picture of your ideal WLPG blend in mind, step 3 will help you consider ways of achieving it as quickly as possible.

STEP 3

Now you have completed step 2, you will know what your ideal WLPG blend looks like. Return to your first sketch in step 1 and sketch out (as shown below) all the 'push' and 'pull' factors that have influenced its shape.

The 'pull' factors are the things that conspired to pull your ideal blend apart, whether they are real or perceived, internal or external, within your control or out of it. The 'push' factors are the things that made it real. Challenge yourself not to make 'reasonable excuses'. For example, if time and money are an issue, how much of a problem is this? If 'family commitments' are stopping you, have you discussed possible ways around this as a family so that everyone can benefit?

PULL
COMMITMENTS
MONEY
WORRY
CONFIDENCE
TIME
AGE

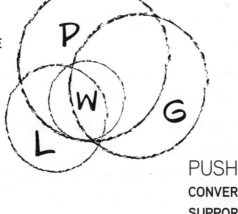

PUSH
CONVERSATIONS
SUPPORT
COURAGE
RESILIENCE
CREATIVITY
RISK

REFLECTION

WHAT IS THE BIGGEST CHALLENGE TO YOUR IDEAL WLPG BLEND?

HOW CAN YOU OVERCOME IT?

WHO CAN HELP YOU AND HOW?

THINK OF THREE SMALL STEPS THAT TOGETHER CAN HELP BRIDGE THE GAP BETWEEN YOUR CURRENT AND IDEAL WLPG SKETCHES.

THINK OF THREE SMALL STEPS THAT CAN PUSH MORE TIME INTO MAKING YOUR IDEAL WLPG CHART A REALITY.

Before planning how to move your WLPG balance from your current sketch to your ideal, it is worth reflecting on the bigger picture.

STEP 4

Your WLPG blend will undoubtably have a connection to and cause a ripple effect on other people's lives. How you perceive your current WLPG blend will be your reality, but other people may see you in a different light. If possible, ask someone close to you to sketch out their view of your current WLPG blend. Both sketches may be similar, but as the example opposite shows, it's possible they will be quite different.

'You will never find time for anything. If you want time you must make it.'

Charles Buxton

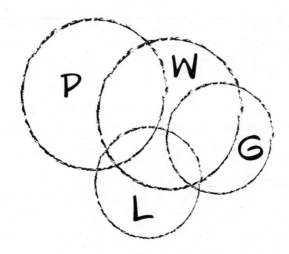

MY WLPG SKETCH

'I've got life in balance.'

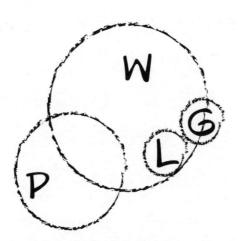

MY PARTNER OR FRIEND'S VIEW

'You're focused too much on work
and don't have any real fun with us.'

REFLECTION

WHAT ARE THE SIMILARITIES AND DIFFERENCES
BETWEEN YOUR TWO SKETCHES?

WHAT CAN YOU DO DIFFERENTLY TO MAKE CHANGES?

HOW CAN YOU HELP THE OTHER PERSON FEEL, THINK
OR SEE THINGS DIFFERENTLY?

Try playing around with the sketches. For example, how can you
create a shared WLPG blend?

'Time is free, but it's priceless.
You can't own it, but you can use it.
You can't keep it, but you can
spend it. Once you've lost it
you can never get it back.'

Harvey McKay

ACT...

So now you have a plan. Today is about identifying where your time is spent, and with whom, where and how you would like it to be devoted. It's easy to continue with habits and patterns that you have followed over a period of time, but it only takes a few minutes and a small amount of determination to shake things up for the better. Let's make today that day.

■ CASE STUDY: Reading your own obituary

This is a true story about two brothers in the middle of their life's week. They had both inherited a multi-national business from their father. Money was no object. They were a new generation of an incredibly wealthy and well-known family.

One brother travelled the world before settling down to utilise his knowledge and training in the family business – of war supplies. His new invention – dynamite – was the bedrock of his future success and wealth. The other brother stayed closer to home, managing and improving the family firm, and then branching out into the oil business and initiating significant research into the industry that brought huge benefits to the world. Alongside this work, he was well known for his humanitarian work and interest in providing for his employees.

Sadly, one day the humanitarian brother had a major accident and was killed. Due to the famous nature of the family, a French newspaper published his obituary. However, in researching his life story the reporter misunderstood which brother had died and wrote the wrong obituary. Opening up the paper, the other brother read his own unfolding life story with sheer terror. He was shocked at how little, other than work and wealth, he had achieved, and at the negativity applied to his achievements. The term 'Merchant of Death' was used. He reflected further and was enormously disturbed by how one-dimensional his career and his life had become and how little of a positive impact his life had made on others. This critical incident of reading his own obituary made him realise the importance of giving something back before it was too late.

This seminal moment totally turned his life on its head for this brother. His name was Nobel, and from his brother's premature death the Nobel Prize was born. This 'tipping point' in Nobel's life had rapidly reduced the size and importance of his work circle and had significantly expanded his giving, which in turn impacted on his sense of happiness and fulfilment – his playing.

> 'Life is like a coin. You can spend it any way you want but you can only spend it once.'
>
> **Lillian Dixon**

If you were to read your own obituary today, what would you regret not seeing in it? More importantly, if you were given six months to live how would you act and think differently from now on in order that you could look back on your life and have no regrets?

THE 5p INVESTMENT

Your task for today is to invest in the most important person of all – yourself. Don't feel this is being selfish; to be there for others you first need to be resourceful and resilient yourself.

1 Grab yourself a five-pence piece. If you can't find one, any coin or note will do. **Before** reading on, make sure the coin is firmly grasped in your right hand so you can't see it.

2 Now, without cheating and looking, describe what is on the coin or note. What pictures or symbols does it have? When was it made? What writing or numbers does it have on it? Many of us struggle to answer these questions, as we just take for granted the things we have every day. In the same way, we may look at ourselves in the mirror every day but we don't necessarily look any deeper – we see our physical reflection but not truly what we reflect.

3 Here is the 5p investment you can apply to your life today. This 5p consists of:

   • Prime skills

   • Passions

   • Purpose

   • Place

   • People

   Have a close look at the four circles you have drawn to represent your life at present. Really focus, and imagine putting a magnifying glass over the area where the circles overlap. This is the time when you're having a combination of fun, learning, giving and maybe even being paid for it – you might even be doing all four at the same time!

4 Looking at the greatest areas of overlap, try answering the questions overleaf. Don't just do this as a mental exercise and move on: get a piece of paper or your notebook and write

down your responses – they will be a valuable reference for your progress later as you move through the steps towards having No Regrets on Sunday.

Prime Skills	What activities are going on in your life right now? Which skills are you currently using? If you wanted to, how could you use these more?
Passions	Are there any real passions or interests you are engaged in at the moment? How can you engage in them more? Do these link with your prime skills, and if so, how?
Purpose	What is making this present time purposeful and meaningful for you? For what purpose would you like to use more of your time?
Place	Where are you when your circles are over-lapping? In work, at home, in a particular environment, or perhaps a special place that's significant for you? Where would you ideally like to spend more of your time?
People	Who are you with when one or more circles overlap? Are there any particular people who make the time special?

In answering these questions, do any patterns emerge?

5 Consider what you have learned from this book so far and how this new knowledge can be applied to your life blend as it stands now; think about how you can use it to get closer to your ideal WLPG blend. Identify how long it should take you

to change your life into your ideal WLPG blend and who you will need to work with to make it happen. Think about the greatest obstacles that prevent you from this achievement and the small steps that can overcome these challenges.

6 Make a commitment today to take small steps each day and regularly check whether they are leading to your ideal blend and the benefits it will bring. Use your notebook to monitor your progress and to regularly redraw your current WLPG blend to ensure that it is moving in a positive direction.

From our experiences at Windmills, in 80 per cent of cases it is the combination of the small steps that make the biggest difference. A key step that you should try to include is to change your perspective of the situation. For example, clients have often said to us:

- *'My situation hasn't changed that much, but the way I think and feel about it has.'*

- *'I've started to think much more about what I'm doing and I now try to use the four dimensions of WLPG – I'm concentrating on growing my play first!'*

- *'I didn't see work as giving before.'*

- *'I only appreciated how much fun it was when it had been taken away from me.'*

Whatever your situation, with a primed mind the more you look for your ideal blend, the more you'll see it.

During the past two days you have equipped yourself with a new mindset and approach to making the most of your week. Tomorrow, we will apply both of these elements to the roles you play. Before we move on, remind yourself of what you have learned today.

TUESDAY: RECAP

- *Recognise each element of WLPG and how they each feature in your life. Ask yourself if you have the blend right for your ideal lifestyle.*

- *Set yourself a realistic deadline in the future by which you could achieve your ideal WLPG blend.*

- *Decide which factors are honestly preventing you achieving your ideal WLPG blend and how you can address them, including discussions with people affected by it.*

'If we did all we were capable of doing, we would literally astonish ourselves.'

Thomas Edison

3

WEDNESDAY
WHO

Find a role you love and you'll
add five days to your weekend

'All the world's a stage and all the men and
women merely players: they have their exits
and their entrances; and one man in his time
plays many parts, his acts being seven ages.'

William Shakespeare

READ...

KNOW WHO YOU ARE AND WHO YOU WANT TO BE

When you looked at yourself in the mirror this morning, what did you see? Who are you and what makes you happy? How do you see yourself at the moment – and is it who you really want to be?

To understand who you are and, for some, who you want to be, you need to think about the many and varied roles you play throughout your life.

THE ROLES YOU PLAY

Try imagining your life as a film in which you play a variety of lead and supporting roles as the drama unfolds, each of which will give you a new identity.

From the moment you're born, you are given the same role as everybody else – that of a child. You play that part instinctively, crying and sleeping at appropriate (and often inappropriate) times, and although this role develops and grows over time, it stays with you throughout much of your life. You will always remain a son or daughter, even as you take on other roles as you move through adulthood.

Depending on your family make-up, background and the environment you grow up in, you also inherit a number of other roles at birth – brother, sister, cousin, step-child, twin, Christian, Muslim, Hindu, Jew and so on.

As you grow up and head off to school you become a student, prefect, peer and perhaps the star of the week. Once you have got through academic life, you enter the world of employment and your work starts to define who you are: your job title gives you a label to describe what you do – dustman, dentist, driver, designer, director, domestic and so on. Aside from work, the home

'A musician must make music, an artist must paint, a poet must write, if he is to be ultimately at peace with himself. What a man can be, he must be.'

Abraham Maslow

also provides myriad roles from cleaner to cook. Your interests, too – from football fan to fisherman, decorator to dancer, or musician to mechanic – have an impact on your lives and the way you live them. In addition, your role in your neighbourhood and local community may also evolve as you grow older and take on new responsibilities – becoming a neighbour, volunteer or perhaps a leader in some capacity.

In all your relationships – personal and professional – you take on many and varied roles, often at the same time, as friends, colleagues, partners or providers. The important thing to remember is that because we play so many different roles throughout the course of our lives, it is vital to understand which ones really matter. If you don't want to end your life looking back with regret at your missed opportunities, take the time now to identify the roles that make you happiest.

■ CASE STUDY: Mirror, mirror on the wall ... do you know yourself at all?

Margaret, a mother in her late forties, looked in the mirror one morning and saw a stranger looking back. She had forgotten who she was! Being bullied over her weight by her older brother and by her wider group of friends and family had stripped

Margaret of all her self-esteem, and when she separated from her husband she lost all her confidence – she couldn't even walk into a pub by herself for fear she would get stuck walking between bar stools. Apart from caring for her two children, the only thing that gave Margaret a feeling of self-worth was cleaning for a friend.

It was at this point that we at Windmills met Margaret for the first time. She had been asked by her friend to volunteer at a social club and we encouraged her to take a massively brave step and go along. By taking on this new role Margaret's confidence blossomed. For the first time in 20 years she had a real sense of purpose, which gave her a new lease of life.

During a number of informal reviews with Margaret held over the next 10 years, it was clear that the social club had become an integral part of her life, and then, with the support of her new friends, she volunteered to organise the club's annual holiday as well as key events throughout the year.

At the same time, one of the club members' mothers was looking in her own mirror, and at the age of 86 she was worried about being able to physically care for her Down's syndrome son, Philip, because the rest of her family had emigrated to Australia and weren't able to help. So Margaret took another leap of faith and offered to become Philip's full-time carer. Twelve months on, Margaret continues to be his guardian and they both regularly visit Philip's mother, who has now moved into a nursing home.

Both mums now look in the mirror and are at ease with who they are, and smile.

SHAPING YOUR IDENTITY

Our identities are shaped by the way we respond to the possibilities and problems we encounter every day. Whether these roles involve working, learning, playing or giving, they all change to some degree as we go through life.

As infants our identities are defined by our names, age and where we live and learn: 'I am ... and I live at ...' As we grow up, our identities are influenced by our peers and education: 'I am a member of this group ...' or 'I am a student at ...' Soon it may become focused around work: 'I am a manager of ...' 'I am an accountant for ...'; or around family life: 'I am a dad with two teenagers.'

As you move through life some of these roles will overtake others in importance. For example, there may be times when you regard your role as a mother or father as more important than your role as an employee, or you may see yourself as a doctor first and a son or daughter second. But remember, the most important role you play is that of being yourself – an individual with your own thoughts, feelings and goals in life. Don't lose sight of the real 'you' underneath all the layers and baggage of your everyday roles; take time on a regular basis to remind yourself of who you really are.

COPING WITH CHANGE

Your portfolio of roles is also continually evolving; some you take up, others you lose or temporarily set aside. At any one moment you may be playing a dozen different roles which require different priorities at different times. This can have a considerable impact, and the unpredictability of life must be taken into account when you plan your futures, so you are prepared for glitches or checks to your goals along the way.

Some of your roles will have a limited lifespan, after which it's time to change or let someone more suited to the position take over. Many you may take for granted and do not appreciate until they disappear or come under threat.

Problems may suddenly enter your working life, such as becoming redundant or retiring, which can remove your role as a colleague and the accompanying social contacts overnight. On a personal level, you may find yourself plunged unexpectedly into a new role – perhaps as a patient, as a carer for a loved one or someone with a disability, or even as a mourner for a departed friend.

FINDING YOUR TRUE ROLE IN LIFE

Some of the many and changing roles you must take on in the course of your life will feel more comfortable than others, but what really matters is whether they are purposeful, fun and fulfilling.

'Your time is limited, so don't waste it living someone else's life.'

Steve Jobs

The key question you need to ask yourself throughout all this is: have you forgotten who you really are? Have you lost your true identity, and lost sight of who you want to focus on being in the future? If you met someone for the first time and they asked 'Who are you? Tell me a bit about yourself', what would be the first thing that you'd say? The key to answering these questions is to understand which roles matter most in the bigger picture, and why. Which roles do you need to put more energy into? And how can you best perform these for the longest time possible?

PRESSURE FROM OTHER PEOPLE

The way other people view us can also have a dramatic effect on how we prioritise our roles and how we see ourselves.

Here we meet the HAVEs, DOs and BEs:

- The HAVEs define who you are by the material wealth you possess as a result of your roles – how much you earn, the type of house you live in, the car you drive, where your luxury holiday is this year, your favourite possessions, and so on.

- The DOs define success by what you do for a living – your status, profession and qualifications.

- The BEs accept you for who you are – a parent, carer, volunteer or homemaker – these people attribute value to you, the person, not your image or your material possessions.

In order to know who you are and who you want to be, it's important to think about who you spend time with – is it the HAVEs, the DOs or BEs? Then ask yourself, which of these would you honestly prefer to be around?

Challenge yourself today to play the important rather than the urgent roles in life. We all have choices, but it is the decisions you make that will determine your happiness and ensure you have No Regrets on Sunday.

What's more important – sending yet another email or spending time with the kids? Who needs you most, your friends or your Hoover? Sit down and assess your priorities; consider which are your dominant roles today and whether you are happy playing them.

■ CASE STUDY: You have to kiss a few frogs before you find your prince

Sarah, a highly driven, 30-year-old home economist, had lost her sparkle and confidence and was quickly becoming lost in her life and unsure of the roles that she wanted to pursue. She approached us at a real low point in her life.

It soon became apparent in discussion that she was living with a very challenging character! The penny dropped that Sarah's partner was the biggest obstacle to her moving forward. Kevin had created a stagnant environment in their relationship; he moaned about everything and did nothing; he boasted about how good he was at various things but in reality never delivered. Effectively, Kevin saw Sarah as a home bird and constantly clipped her wings.

A combination of this toxic relationship, together with a stressful work role which required a tremendous amount of travel in order to climb to the top of the tree, greatly affected Sarah's health and well-being. As a result she put on weight and was regularly off work with stress. This unhappy situation was compounded by friends who, one by one, got married and started families.

With our support Sarah created a picture for her future which contained four dramatic new elements: a new house, new location, new job and new partner. Not one to put off difficult decisions once they had become clear to her, she decided to change two or three roles all at the same time. The first being to leave her partner, the second to put her house on the market and the third to research a new job in the South of England.

Rather than letting someone else control her life, Sarah at last took ownership of her future. She has since found her ideal role in a healthcare company, through which she met her husband and the father to her child. She now works part-time and loves her new roles.

Her message is simple: 'Be honest with yourself, and if you feel trapped or caged in a toxic relationship, whether at home or work – life's too short. If you can't change it, get out of it. And remember – what's the point of winning the rat race if you remain a rat!'

'Our achievements of today are but the sum total of our thoughts of yesterday. You are today where the thoughts of yesterday have brought you and you will be tomorrow where the thoughts of today take you.'

Blaise Pascal

THINK...

THE STORY OF YOUR LIFE

Imagine that every day when you get home from work you slump down in front of the TV. But tonight, instead of watching your favourite soap or a football match, you find yourself watching an omnibus version of the story of your life to date. Faced with your life before you, can you identify which roles you have been playing so far?

CHILD	COLLEAGUE
FRIEND	SHOPPER
PARTNER	HOME-MAKER
MEMBER	CHAUFFEUR
NEIGHBOUR	PROFESSIONAL
CITIZEN	ADDICT
VOLUNTEER	POLITICIAN
WIDOW	JOBSEEKER
CARER	DISABLED
LISTENER	PRACTITIONER
STUDENT	CRIMINAL
EMPLOYER	COMMUNICATOR
HANDYPERSON	EMPLOYEE
BOSS	LEADER
MENTOR	LEARNER
MYSELF	SUPPORTER

COMMUTER	EXPERT
REFUGEE	BROTHER
GRANDPARENT	SISTER
DIVORCEE	GIVER
LOVER	TRUSTEE
BELIEVER	COOK
RELATIVE	DIRECTOR
RETIREE	EXPLORER
BREADWINNER	ASSOCIATE
INVESTOR	FUNDRAISER
MANAGER	SOCIALISER
CHAMPION	SPECIALIST
TEACHER	CONSULTANT
ENTREPRENEUR	ADVOCATE
SINGLE	CLEANER
PARENT	INVENTOR
STORYTELLER	DEVELOPER
ADMINISTRATOR	COACH
TRAVELLER	MEDIATOR
TEAM PLAYER	PIONEER
PUBLIC SERVANT	PATIENT
BUSINESS PERSON	CUSTOMER

Follow the steps below so that you can identify who you have been until now. This will help you to decide which parts of your life you want or need to change to be the person you ultimately want to be.

1   Look at the list of roles above and think about which ones you've played in the last month or so.

2 From these, pick the seven main roles that are most relevant to your life at the moment – the ones that take up most of your time. List them in the first column of the storyboard opposite. Feel free to add or change the titles of any of these roles to suit your situation.

3 Next, think about how much time and energy you put into each role. In column 2 rank this from 1 to 7 (1 = the most, 7 = the least). Avoid giving any roles equal rankings.

4 Look at how important each role is to you at the moment and rank them from 1 to 7 in column 3.

5 Finally, put yourself in the shoes of the person related to this role. If they were asked how well they see you performing this role, what would your score be and why? Write your scores in column 4 – A* being outstanding through to F – a complete flop!

REFLECTION

SO WHAT'S THIS TELLING YOU ABOUT THE ROLES YOU ARE PLAYING IN LIFE?

ARE YOU SPENDING PRIME TIME ON THE ROLE YOU FEEL IS MOST IMPORTANT AND IS YOUR PERFORMANCE RATING IN IT A*?

WHERE ARE YOU DOING WELL?

WHERE ARE THE TENSIONS?

WHERE COULD YOU DO EVEN BETTER? WHAT CHANGES DO YOU NEED TO MAKE?

MY STORYBOARD

ROLE	TIME/ ENERGY	IMPORTANCE	PERFORMANCE

Remember, we all look at life through our own lens. The challenge is that at any moment we only see half of the true picture – and this is usually whatever's right in front of our own camera. Even when we turn our camera round, there will always be something else going on behind it.

The truth can only be seen by that bigger camera looking down from above at the whole picture, the camera that picks up the broader thread, makes connections between scenes and sees how the story unfolds and finally ends. The next stage of this exercise gives you a chance to operate this third camera.

TIME TO CHANGE THE PLOT

You may now be conscious that you need to rearrange or rewrite your roles in life, whether this is an immediate scene change or a gradual rehearsal for a more important part you wish or need to play. To do this, you might need to change the PLOT. PLOT is a simple process that can help you to work out what you need to change:

PICK

What new roles, attitudes, behaviours, values or skills do you need to pick up?

LOSE

What negative baggage or behaviour, commitments or roles do you need to lose?

OPEN

How can you be more open to new possibilities? Who can open new opportunities for you?

TURN

What twists and turns might you encounter, and how can you turn them to your advantage?

Pick one role that you'd love to expand or improve. Focus clearly on one small step – it may be as simple as having a conversation, saying no to a request, or creating some 'me time'. Don't worry about playing the ideal role the first time round – practice makes perfect. Remember, it's up to you to play the starring role in your life story – no one else. Keep to your own script, and never lose the PLOT!

■ CASE STUDY: Play your cards right

Each of us may be at our own time of day in the week of our life, but we will all have loved ones on different days.

Ros was a highly focused and successful director of a well-known social enterprise that was engaged in environmental recycling. She attended one of our workshops at Windmills and worked on the life roles exercise. As she talked through the activity with a complete stranger on the course she realised she was shocked at the findings. On completing this exercise it dawned on her that the most important person in her life, her mother, was the person to whom she gave least time and energy. Even when she was in the same room as her mother, Ros suffered from presenteeism – meaning that she would sit with her but her mind would be on a work issue rather than listening to what her mother was saying.

Ros drove home from the workshop in tears, as she had realised that she had to change her PLOT. That day she took steps to change the thing that was making her most unhappy and committed to buying a holiday home in North Wales. She promised herself that she would spend two weekends a month there with her mother. Without a TV and, more importantly, her laptop, Ros and her mum had a fabulous number of nights playing cards together. For the first time Ros really got to know who her mum was and how her own life story had unfolded.

I met Ros several years later and she had since sold the holiday home. She cursed me with a jest that I cost her thousands of pounds as she had bought the home at the peak of the market and had sold it at the lowest point. But with a smile she said it was the best investment she had ever made. She'll never forget sitting with her mum and a glass of red wine, playing rummy.

We all get dealt a unique set of cards in life, but it's not the cards you are dealt with that affect your future; it's how you choose to play them and who you choose to play them with. The choice is yours. Are you prepared to gamble or even bluff and pretend you have cards you don't actually have? And who do you choose to play them with? The danger of holding your cards too close to your chest is that other people will not be able to see and share them with you.

ACT...

TIME FOR YOUR PERFORMANCE REVIEW

Your task for today is to find out the truth about the roles you play. You've had a chance to rate yourself in each role, but how accurate are your grades?

1   Make sure you don't lose sight of the 'me' role, as this is the one that will influence all the others. Sit down for five minutes and carry out a review on yourself by completing the following sentences:

I'm someone who:

- Feels passionate about ....

- Believes in ....

- Loves ....

- Has a conviction to ....

- Gets most fun and fulfilment from ....

- Hates ....

- Dreams of ....

- Believes I make a difference by ....

- And I demonstrate this by ....

Our roles in life are most successful and satisfying when they utilise our strengths and likes, so use your answers above to check that your key roles synchronise with who you are where possible.

2 Now take a role that really matters to you and identify the person or people who benefit from or relate most to this role. For example, if the role is 'son' or 'daughter', the person would be one of your parents. If it is 'employee', you should choose your line manager. Now answer the following questions as if from their point of view – what do you think their answers and reactions would be?

- What do you value most about our relationship?

- What do you look for in me or expect from me?

- If you were honest enough to give me some feedback on my role as a ..., on what criteria would you base your views?

- How well would I rate on each (A* to F)?

- Where do you feel I need to improve?

- What steps could I take to be the best I can be?

- Is there anything we could do together to improve my performance in this role?

Immediately you will see a clearer picture of how effective this role is and whether or not your input relates directly to its success.

3 Now, if you can, approach the person and open up a conversation. Create the space to talk, ideally face to face, but if distance is a problem, do it on the phone. If today is not covenient, try to schedule a time later in the week. Your task is to find out what this person really thinks and feels about

how you play this specific role, using the questions above as a guide.

The goal in this exercise is to question and listen, not to judge, react or even try to turn the tables on the other person. Whatever comes out from this exercise, make sure you thank them at the end!

4 Now reflect on a couple of things. Firstly, did the person you spoke to use the same criteria for measuring your performance as you thought they would? What are they looking, needing or wanting from you? For example, one mum thought her teenage son would want her to always be there for him, but in fact his main criteria at the time were 'is my football kit clean?' and 'can you drive me to the game?' One line manager on our programme also failed to fully understand the needs of one of his team. Due to this 'conversation gap' he thought his employee wanted more pay, but in fact she really needed a better work/life balance to make her happier at work. Finally, how well did this person rate your performance? Did they give you any helpful feedback to help you improve your score?

One of the key factors influencing the quality of the roles we play is whether they make full use of the skills we love using and are good at. This is the theme for Thursday, and the next step towards having No Regrets on Sunday. But before we move on, remind yourself of who you really are and want to be.

You're now halfway through the week, and hopefully by now you should be well on your way to gaining a new perspective on life. If you are taking in these new ideas, by the time you finish this book you will be able to look back on your week with much more satisfaction when Sunday comes.

WEDNESDAY: RECAP

- *Recognise the myriad of roles you play, but take time out every now and again to remind yourself of who you really are.*

- *Decide which of the roles you are currently playing are important to you and have a place in your life to allow you to have No Regrets on Sunday.*

- *Make time to change the PLOT – the only person who can change yourself is you.*

'And in the end, it's not the years in your life that count, it's the life in your years.'

Abraham Lincoln

4

THURSDAY
TALENTS

You're a unique person with more skills than you think

'Hide not your talents, they for use were made. What's a sundial in the shade?'

Benjamin Franklin

READ...

YOU ARE UNIQUE

When you turn on the radio and surf the various stations, have you ever marvelled at how every piece of music is so different – from hip-hop to house, country to classical, or rock to rhythm 'n' blues? Yet amazingly all music is created from the same seven core notes – the diverse sounds and styles come from the varying ways in which they are combined. Again, when you survey the huge variety of books that line the shelves of a bookshop, from fiction to non-fiction, science to sport or business to biography, does it strike you that every one uses just 26 letters of the alphabet? It's simply the order in which they are used that differs.

> 'Genius is the gold in the mine; talent is the miner who works and brings it out.'
>
> **Lady Blessington**

The same principle applies when you look at people and the individual talents or skills they possess. In fact, we all have similar families of skills at our fingertips, and what makes each of us unique is the way in which we inter-relate them.

SPOTTING YOUR PRIME SKILLS

With so many combinations of skills at our disposal, we need to identify which can be the most useful to us. Luckily, there are two clear clues for spotting these prime skills (which I'll come on to in a minute. When you've picked out the skills you love using – and are really good at – you need to apply them in areas that make you come alive.

The first clue is how much we love using a particular skill – whether we're good at it or not. We can easily spot a skill we love because time simply flies when we're using it. (If we're stuck using skills we hate, time drags and we end up clock-watching and wishing it was time to stop or go home.)

The second clue lies in how good we are at a particular skill. The better we are at something – whether it's laying bricks, dealing with figures or running a business – the more likely someone is to pay us for doing it.

So your prime skills are simply those you love using and are best at. In fact, you love them so much you might still use them even if you weren't being paid to do so.

IT'S YOUR CHOICE

We may carry a number of skills through life with us, but we have a choice as to which ones we'd really love to use.

Consider these three questions:

1 The average adult has approximately 500 skills: from this number can you spot the seven you love most and are best at?

2 Are you making the most of these skills for a purpose that you are passionate about?

3 Are you proactively seeking and creating opportunities in your daily working, learning, playing and giving to maximise your prime skills?

We asked thousands of people these questions. Most fell at the first hurdle because they'd never sat down and thought about their prime skills, which explains why so many people tell us that they feel underemployed and undervalued in their jobs. The easy option for not being happy at work is to blame your employer, but ultimately it's down to the individual to discover which of their own skills they love and where they can use them.

Each of us is unique in the way we combine our prime skills with something we are passionate about and which matters to us. Wouldn't it be great to answer 'Yes' to each of these three questions? Just imagine what it would mean if everyone we knew answered yes, yes, yes! Think how productive our workforce would be, what wonderfully positive relationships we'd all enjoy, and what strong communities we would all live in!

■ CASE STUDY: Transferring your army of skills

At the age of 21, Stuart gave his life to a career in the army. Together with his sisters, Stuart followed in his father's footsteps – if he was a stick of rock he would have 'officer' written all the way through him. While back from tour he met his future wife at a nightclub and a couple of years later they got married, but all his focus remained on his army career. However, things changed dramatically after they had their first child.

Stuart was at his wife's side for her birth, but within two weeks had to return back to a tour in Bosnia. It was six weeks later that his friend sent him a DVD of his daughter, Erin. The euphoria of receiving a gift from home was replaced by the shock of how quickly Erin had changed in such a short time. Stuart saw in 30 seconds how time could flash by. He realised that if he carried on doing what he'd always done he would get what he'd always got – a daughter that he'd never know!

Watching the DVD created a fork in Stuart's career path. It was time to change the tour otherwise he would end up in a pretty sad place called 'Regrets'.

Sitting down with Stuart, we helped him create a new route which maximised his transferable skills in finance, scenario planning and people management. Rather than taking a splatter-gun approach, Stuart decided to target his efforts on a career within the actuarial industry. He made an informed decision on the basis that it valued the skills he loved using and it was a growth area.

Finally, the industry had major businesses which were within 1½ hours' commute of home. Having found his target, we then agreed an action plan to maximise his chances of hitting it. The approach wasn't the ready, aim, fire of a rifle shot, it was more like the ready, fire, aim of a missile. Stuart had to get intelligence on the ground as to where his key target employers were moving in terms of future markets and skills needs, and which companies were most closely aligned to his values of integrity, hard work and a sense of professionalism.

Having conducted a range of information interviews with leading actuarial firms, Stuart seized an opportunity which hit 80 per cent of his criteria, the only problem being a two-hour commute. Stuart was prepared to compromise to get his foot in the door and he committed to at least five further years of part-time study. More importantly, he didn't stop the information interviewing process and two years later his persistence paid off. A niche actuarial company within ten minutes from home had kept his details on file since he had carried out one of his ongoing information interviews, and without even advertising the opportunity, they approached him.

Five years on, Stuart has qualified. He is now in a new role in his organisation which maximises the relationship-building and people-management skills he loved using in the army.

Stuart realised that his family and home were most important to him, reviewed his portfolio of skills and transferred them to a place that met his life goals. So what is most important to you, and how can you use your skills to help you achieve this?

LET YOUR SKILLS SHINE

Imagine your skills as a unique set of diamonds; they dazzle and shine in the light but lie dull and forgotten when shut away in their case. In the same way, your skills are always there, but sometimes you lose sight of them. So it is important to bring them out and use them on a regular basis if you want to introduce some sparkle into your life. They are precious gifts that shouldn't be wasted.

'With ordinary talents and extraordinary perserverance, all things are attainable.'

Sir Thomas Fowell Buxton

CHECK THAT MINDSET!

So what's stopping you from seeing clearly these precious gifts that you have to offer – your own prime skills? And are you making the most of them for a purpose that you are passionate about?

If not, perhaps you are saying to yourself, 'I can't, that's all well and good but', 'I have no choice', or even 'I can't be bothered'. This is where you need to check your mindset and remember what you learned on Monday about changing those old habits.

Remind yourself that in the end it is up to you and you do have choices if you manage your time correctly – this is where what we talked about on Tuesday can help.

If you look at your WLPG you may be able to find a way to create ways of blending those four key areas of your life – working, learning, playing and giving. Think about the choices WLPG provide. Your ideal may be to get paid for your prime skills, but that plan may not be possible at the moment.

So Plan B could be to learn more about your skills and develop them further. And why stop at Plan B? Plan C could be to use them more in a social context, while Plan D might be to explore voluntary work opportunities. Once you start thinking about it, the possibilities are endless.

Finally, remember what you learned in yesterday's exercises about the changing roles you play in life. Why not think about all the roles you play in your life and hope to play in the future? Then consider how you are going to use your prime skills to play your part effectively throughout the rest of your week.

As the example on the next page shows, one of the most valuable ways of boosting your confidence, letting your skills shine, developing new talents and creating new possibilities is through volunteering. It's free, purposeful and gives things back with interest. If you had two hours free this week, who would you love to give that time to? If you don't have any time available, try making the most of what you're already doing – it could be a project opportunity at work or helping friends and family.

'Act as if what you do makes a difference. It does.'

William James

ENTERPRISE SKILLS

FUNDRAISING
for holidays
NETWORKING
with Social Services
LEADING
weekends away

PEOPLE SKILLS

LISTENING
to people's worries
HELPING
boost confidence
BEFRIENDING
being an advocate

PRACTICAL SKILLS

DRIVING
less able members
HANDLING
wheelchairs
PRODUCING
name badges

I ONLY VOLUNTEER
at a club for adults
with learning difficulties

CREATIVE SKILLS

CREATING
arts and crafts
DESIGNING
group activities
VISIONING
the club's future

EXPLORING SKILLS

RESEARCHING
members' needs
INTERVIEWING
the families
OBSERVING
personal growth

PROCESSING SKILLS

ADMINISTRATING
databases
DEVELOPING
a website
COLLECTING
subscriptions

■ **CASE STUDY: Learning to eat with 10-foot chopsticks**

There were once two dining rooms, each with a wonderful banquet. One was as sad as can be, the other full of people laughing, singing and chatting. Each room comprised people eating with giant 10-foot chopsticks. In the first, the guests were trying desperately to feed themselves without any joy. In the second they were happily feeding each other!

Chloe and Joe had worked as colleagues together for over 10 years in a large public-sector organisation. They had got on reasonably well over that time and enjoyed working with one another as they shared the same values, despite having very different skills mixes.

Joe was a creative person with lots of fresh ideas and thinking but he lacked the realism to make them happen, while Chloe's strength was to turn strategic ideas into practical action. She loved developing relationships and the systems needed to keep those going, while Joe was keen on exploring new opportunities in an enterprising way.

As can happen in large organisations, a decision was taken from on high to close the department the two colleagues were working in. Chloe's skill mix was seen as crucial to the future of the organisation, and so she was offered redeployment; however, Joe was seen in a different light and he knew that he was headed for redundancy.

Another option, though, was for the two colleagues to take a brave step and combine their forces to establish their own business. This idea had been discussed on a number of occasions in the time they had worked together but both had never really believed it would happen.

After a number of conversations with their families, Chloe and Joe decided to team up and combine their strengths to establish a new venture. Two years on, the business has grown from strength to strength and their combination of skills remains a key to their success.

So, the question is, are you trying to feed yourself with 10-foot chopsticks or are you getting round the table with like-minded colleagues, friends or business partners to share your complementary skills and talents? Remember, the skills you absolutely hate using and are terrible at may be exactly the same skills that others love using.

'E raka te maui,
e raka te katau.
(A community can
use all the skills
of its people.)'
Maori proverb

THINK...

PLAY YOUR PART

To play your full part, make your own unique contribution and have absolutely no regrets in life you need to pinpoint your prime skills, stay focused on them and combine them in various ways. Like the core notes that combine to make up every piece of music imaginable, you are equipped with a core family of skills and talents that you can combine in countless ways to bring harmony to your life. The following exercise will provide you with two simple steps to Play Your Part in Life:

STEP 1 – STARTING TODAY ON THE RIGHT NOTE

1   Think of all the 'magic moments' in your life so far – your big successes, the happy times, those singular moments where time has stood still and you've really come alive. Explore all aspects of your life – your working, learning, playing and giving. Think too of your moments of despair and the challenges you've overcome. Use hindsight to recognise that some of our greatest gifts in life come poorly wrapped. If you have time, you may want to jot these down for future reference.

2   On the following pages, look down each of the six families of skills and tick in the first column those you absolutely love using. Use your ideas in Point 1 to trigger the skills you enjoy.

Don't worry about how good you are at them at this stage, we're just trying to establish what you enjoy.

3   Now go back to the skills you've ticked and in the second column tick all those you are good at. These are your prime skills.

4   In the third column, tick any skills that you think you need to develop further. This may be to make you more employable in the future, perform better in your role or get you closer to your ideal work/life blend.

5   Feel free to create a seventh family of your specialist skills if it is not covered within the skills portfolio.

6   Finally, you might want to highlight any 'bum notes' – those skills you absolutely hate and need to dump, delegate or delay using at all costs.

7   So how are you going to start on the right note today? In the next hour, which one prime skill could you use more, and how? In which areas do you need to practise more (your development skills)? Which tunes do you need to stop playing?

LOVE USING
GOOD AT
DEVELOP

PEOPLE SKILLS

RELATING

Creating rapport
Building relationships
Valuing others

COMMUNICATING

Presenting
Listening
Liaising

HELPING ○○○

Supporting
Volunteering
Sharing

EMPOWERING ○○○

Encouraging
Developing others
Inspiring

MANAGING ○○○

Realising potential
Optimising
Co-ordinating

UNDERSTANDING

Having perspective
Empathising
Valuing differences

TEAMWORKING

Working collectively
Sharing skills
Balancing interests

		LOVE USING	GOOD AT	DEVELOP

PROCESSING SKILLS

PROCESSING
Carrying out procedures
Following instructions
Working structurally and
systematically
○ ○ ○

ADMINISTRATING
Overseeing
Completing
Delivering
○ ○ ○

MAINTAINING
Controlling quality
Managing information
Updating
○ ○ ○

COMPUTING
Utilising up-to-date
IT packages
Technical IT skills
Setting up IT systems
○ ○ ○

WORDS & PICTURES
Writing
Drawing
Translating
○ ○ ○

REVIEWING
Performance
Evaluating
Action planning
○ ○ ○

FINANCES
Budgeting
Accounting
Auditing
○ ○ ○

LOVE USING
GOOD AT
DEVELOP

ENTERPRISE SKILLS

LEADING
Directing people
Planning and targets
Driving change
○ ○ ○

NETWORKING
Support community
Growing relationships
Sharing your talents
○ ○ ○

STRATEGISING
Forecasting
Researching
Business planning
○ ○ ○

SELLING
Negotiating
Influencing
Following up
○ ○ ○

SELF-MANAGING
Motivating self
Seizing opportunities
Promoting self
○ ○ ○

CHAMPIONING
Advocating
Pioneering
Promoting new ideas
○ ○ ○

MARKETING
Assessing needs
Generating possibilities
Enhancing profile
○ ○ ○

PRACTICAL SKILLS	LOVE USING	GOOD AT	DEVELOP
OPERATING Precision working Using machinery Using multi-media	○	○	○
CO-ORDINATING Multi-tasking Organising Delegating	○	○	○
SENSING Hearing Seeing Touching	○	○	○
FIXING Servicing Repairing Maintaining	○	○	○
WELL-BEING Exercising Relaxing Thinking positively	○	○	○
PRODUCING Crafting Making Constructing	○	○	○
NURTURING Tending Growing Fostering	○	○	○

LOVE USING
GOOD AT
DEVELOP

EXPLORING SKILLS

EXPLORING
Investigating
Identifying possibilities
Generating alternatives
○ ○ ○

INTERVIEWING
Questioning
Listening
Selecting
○ ○ ○

OBSERVING
Assessing people
Comparing
Learning from data
○ ○ ○

LEARNING
Reflecting
Experimenting
Improving
○ ○ ○

RESEARCHING
Gathering information
Collecting and recording
Drawing conclusions
○ ○ ○

SOLVING PROBLEMS
Analysing
Seeing patterns
Developing solutions
○ ○ ○

REALISING POTENTIAL
Uncovering personal
strengths, passions
and purpose
Seeking feedback
Taking action
○ ○ ○

	LOVE USING	GOOD AT	DEVELOP

CREATIVE SKILLS

THINKING LATERALLY ○○○

Taking fresh perspectives
Using intuition
Seeing new angles

DESIGNING ○○○

Implementing new ideas
Developing products
Drafting

MEDIA ○○○

Using multi-media
creatively
Exploiting different media
Art and design

ADAPTING ○○○

Enhancing
Translating
Combining

CONNECTING ○○○

Seeing links
Synthesising
Building on ideas

CREATING ○○○

Innovating
Developing
Conceiving

VISIONING ○○○

Imagining the future
Seeing the whole picture
Turning failure into success

STEP 2 – STRIKING THE RIGHT CHORD

Remember, it's not the single notes that define the tune you play in life, it's the combination of these notes that counts.

1 Highlight your top seven prime skills and prioritise them in terms of how much you'd love to use them in an ideal day. The first skill is the one you love to use the most, even if you weren't paid to use it. If you don't have seven prime skills, don't worry – simply look at all the skills you love using.

2 Consider each of your seven prime skills and ask yourself the question: 'To what extent does my work currently maximise this skill?'

3 You may want to repeat or change the exercise, asking the broader question: 'How far does my life as a whole maximise this skill?'

For some people this exercise reinforces how closely work matches their prime skills and they quickly become aware of how much they take for granted. For others it brings about a dramatic realisation that it's time for a complete career or life change.

So what are you going to do to begin striking a better chord today and how will you orchestrate the rest of your week? For many of us the answer lies in playing in the right venue to the right audience – you might be taking a chance by playing heavy metal at a Women's Institute fundraising event, but you might risk being arrested if you did the same in a quiet library.

Remind yourself that you are an extremely talented, unique individual. It's now time to play your part as loudly as you can.

Remember, it's your unique combination of skills that helps you play your part in life, so try to create working, learning, playing and giving opportunities that blend your prime skills. You might do this to negotiate a secondment in marketing to utilise your exploring, creative and processing skills, or perhaps when volunteering to help organise a summer holiday to develop your planning, fundraising and caring skills.

■ CASE STUDY: The slop bucket approach to life

Imagine carrying a huge slop bucket through life with you. As you progress through work experience, volunteering, your first job, secondments, promotions and time out, as well as pastimes, you slop all your skills into the one bucket. While this is great in some ways, because you have more to offer future employers, it also means the bucket gets heavier and heavier as more stuff goes into it. The danger is that we lose focus on what we've got in there and don't sift through the bucket to grasp the skills we love using.

Kathryn was a Contracts Manager in a public-sector agency. Every time she did the skills exercise in this book her love of cooking rose to the surface. Kathryn had always had a pipe dream of setting up her own cookery business; however, in her day job, which paid the bread and butter, she was particularly good at project management. Quickly, she became the project management guru, and before she knew it she was seduced into managing the whole process. While she had become an expert in negotiating, contracting, budgeting, target setting and evaluation, she had ceased to enjoy this family of skills. In fact, she began to hate them!

Kathryn's situation worsened when the agency cut 30 per cent of its staff. Her workload doubled and the learning, playing and giving areas in her life virtually disappeared. Over the next two years Kathryn's passion for cooking kept being covered by more helpings of project management. We're not talking nouvelle cuisine here but massive dollops of school dinners – bucket loads in fact. The only thing keeping Kathryn going was the promise of a gold clock from her employer and her friends constantly telling her that she'd be stupid to leave a secure job and give up an excellent pension in such a poor economic climate.

Who knows whether it was the push away from a challenging role or the pull towards an exciting new venture (or a combination of the two) that tipped the bucket, but Kathryn finally decided to trade in her bucket for a new bowl and create her own cake-baking business. While still at the early stages, she has already established a growing client base, including her son's hockey team, friends' weddings and catering for conferences for ex-colleagues. Based in her kitchen at home, Kathryn's next brave step is to rent a bigger catering unit. Her half-baked idea is now rising rapidly!

Kathryn's message is simple: 'When you finally kick the bucket, how much unwanted, unfulfilling slop will fall out?' Take time today to sift through the skills you love using and are good at, and dump some of the slop!

ACT...

MAXIMISE YOUR PRIME SKILLS

You're an amazing person with a unique portfolio of over 500 skills and talents, but what are you doing today to use and develop them?

Your task for today is to create the opportunity to further use, develop, grow or share the skills you love. Our belief and experience shows that it's important to focus and build on what you love doing rather than where you feel there is a gap.

1 Pick one or two skills that you love using and you would really like to spend more time thinking about and developing today.

2 Using your WLPG circles drawn on Tuesday's exercise as a guide, take action today to maximise these skills. The examples below may stimulate some fresh ideas for you which could be worked on over the next day.

WORKING

- Plan to talk to your boss about how you could use these one or two skills more.

- Create a project, task or secondment that uses them more.

- Share these skills with colleagues.

LEARNING

- Learn more about these skills – whether formally or informally.

- Learn from others, perhaps find a role model.

- Learn how you can transfer these skills to other places, environments, and sectors.

PLAYING

- Use these skills with friends and family.

- Link them to something you feel really passionate about.

- Have fun with them, travel with them, improve your well-being with them.

GIVING

- Volunteer somewhere that you can use these skills.

- Share or teach them to others.

- Find others to collaborate with to make a greater difference.

Consider the activity you completed on Wednesday and think about any of these roles that may provide you with the chance to maximise your skills.

You may now be in a better position to answer the question: 'Can you spot the seven skills you love using and are good at?' Friday will help you to look at what true fulfilment means for you, but before we go on, consider again whether you are maximising your talents for a purpose you are passionate about.

'You miss 100% of the shots you don't take.'

Wayne Gretzky

THURSDAY: RECAP

- *Play to your strengths. Identify which combination of skills you love using most.*

- *Challenge yourself. Are you maximising these prime skills on a regular basis in your working, learning, playing and giving?*

- *Uncover people and opportunities that can help you have more fun with your skills, share them with others, and combine them to make a greater difference than you could do by yourself.*

'Life gains meaning in places where your deep gladness and the world's deep hunger meet.'

Dick Bolles

5

FRIDAY
FULFILMENT

You can achieve just
about anything if it matters
enough to you

'Not everything that can be counted counts.
And not everything that counts can be counted.'
Albert Einstein

READ...

FULL OR FULFILLED?

Everyone looks forward to Friday: the day that traditionally marks the end of the working week and the beginning of the weekend, which is for most people the time to do all the enjoyable stuff that has been squeezed out of the previous days.

However, it's worrying to think that millions of people will spend 40+ years of their working lives literally wishing their week away until they can say 'thank goodness it's Friday'. The longed-for Friday night then finishes in a flash, Saturday is spent recovering from the events of the night before or the previous week, and Sunday finds people planning for the week ahead.

So is time simply passing you by as you sleepwalk through life, or are you making the most of it? Is each week totally 'full' or truly 'fulfilling'? Okay, we all have those mundane chores to do, whether it is cleaning, DIY or paying bills, but just think what a Friday night would be like if you had reached it with five days of fulfilling activity under your belt.

So, how can you bring more fulfilment into each and every day? Quite simply, you just need to wake up to the things that bring passion and purpose to your life, and spend more time and energy on doing the things that are really meaningful to you. Focus on what is worthwhile, rather than worthless.

The best way to bring fulfilment and meaning into your life is by making optimum use of your talents and skills. The key lies in recognising which skills you love using and are really good at (see

Thursday), and then deciding how you can apply them to a purpose you're passionate about. You will then find you gain the pay-offs that matter most to you.

Luckily, we can combine our passions and purposes in many different ways – through working, learning, playing and giving (see Tuesday). For example, we can link our passion for music with a charity dear to our heart by playing at a fundraising event. Or we can connect our enthusiasm for a particular sport with a real motivation to empower young people, perhaps by coaching the local children's football or netball team.

It is the combination of these passions and purposes across the whole of our lives that makes each of us uniquely fulfilled. It is the small daily activities as well as the bigger life changes that make all the difference. Probably the smallest step you can take is to look at yourself in the mirror and think about what brings a smile to your face.

'Happiness is the meaning and the purpose of life, the whole aim and end of human existence.'

Aristotle

BE TRUE TO YOURSELF

Enjoying the simple things in life is often what gives us the greatest pleasure. However, pressure from our peers and the media can often mean we develop a skewed outlook on life. There may be some of us who know in our heart of hearts that we are spending more money than we have on things we don't need in order to impress people we don't even like – all in the search for so-called happiness. Happiness is very personal; so what does it honestly mean to you?

We are all human beings and so, when life's all about having or doing, we can lose sight of simply being. For instance, we may change our clothes, jobs, homes or cars, but underneath we fundamentally remain the same.

So, ask yourself now, have you lost the capacity to simply be and enjoy being yourself? If you're not sure, here are some simple questions to help you decide:

- How many times did you smile last week?

- When was the last time you laughed so much your ribs ached?

- Have you stopped today and been thankful for the simple things in life?

- Did you get up this morning full of enthusiasm for the day ahead?

- Are you spending time focusing on what you don't have – or are you happy with who you are and what you have?

If you struggle with any of these questions, it's time to ask yourself 'What does true fulfilment and happiness mean for me?' and, 'How can I create more of it today?'

■ CASE STUDY: Riding the wave

We all have fractures running through our lives. They may be major traumas, or separations, a combination of challenges in our working, learning, playing and giving, or simply major distortions in the way we view the world around us.

Mary was in her late teens when she received a double blow that sent shock waves through her life. She lost both her father and brother within 12 months of each other. The ensuing tsunami totally engulfed her; she felt dazed, battered and bruised. Her confidence had been washed away and she'd lost all sense of direction. But as with any natural disaster, there were also signs of hope; whether tremendous acts of kindness, young lives saved in the rubble or communities coming together to rebuild and heal.

Mary's life was no different. After a period of devastation she changed her studies from IT, which she had never really enjoyed, to follow in her brother's footsteps as a chiropodist. She spent many years as an outreach health worker in the local community. Mary gained a new sense of purpose, combining her technical chiropody skills with an ability to relate to and communicate with elderly people, who for the most part had her as their only visitor that day.

But this wasn't enough for Mary: by chance, she fell into one of our programmes. In a light-bulb moment she realised she could combine her listening and interpersonal skills with a passion for health and well-being, together with empowering young people. She secured funding and retrained as a careers adviser. Sadly, Mary's foundations were shaken once more. Her mother, whom she was extremely close to, died of cancer. Floods of emotion came back and it took several more years for her to get back on to an even keel. A fundraising 'race for life', where she saw so many other people with their loved ones' names written on their t-shirts,

> 'The purpose of life is … to be useful, to be honourable, to be compassionate, to have it make some difference that you have lived and lived well.'
>
> **Ralph Waldo Emerson**

was a key moment for Mary. She decided there and then to focus on the quality she loved most about her mum and commit to living it every day. In this way, she reasoned, her mum would never die. That quality was one of showing care and compassion to other people. Mary now volunteers in her local community, helps in the local primary school and is a trustee of a new children's charity.

For Mary, pain has provided a pathway to a new purpose. She has learned to ride the wave.

FIND YOUR FULFILMENT FACTOR

Imagine drawing a graph of your levels of happiness over the past week, month, year or even life as a whole. Just like a weather chart it will have its highs (sunny periods), its lows (dark clouds of depression) and its cloudy days (when nothing really happens).

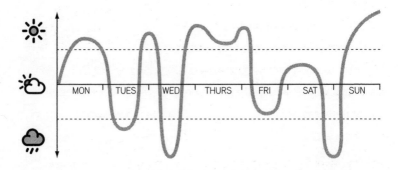

Glance up at the sky. There will be a unique arrangement of clouds and sunshine in a blue or grey sky – and it will never look quite the same again. This pattern of change occurs in our lives too.

The clue to bringing more fun, happiness and lasting content-ment into our lives lies in the way we think about and manage each of the three segments – the highs, the lows and the cloudy days. Let's start with the phase in which most of us hope to spend the majority of our time – the highs.

HOLD ON TO YOUR HIGHS

When you look at the high points in people's lives it's amazing to see how quickly their happiness chart begins to plunge down.

All too often our magic moments are brief intervals of blazing sunshine that don't last long enough. Whether it's dancing with friends on a Friday night, an amazing academic achievement or success at work, or fulfilling a personal passion that briefly brings you alive – these events are often only momentary. So, in order to get more fun into our lives we all need to look at creative ways through which we can get more highs in our week and can make them last longer.

The 'Think' section in this chapter will challenge you to do this by finding purposes and passions that are fun, will energise you and will also have a lasting meaning.

> 'When written in Chinese the word 'crisis' is composed of two characters. One represents danger. The other represents opportunity.'
>
> **John F. Kennedy**

DON'T OVERLOOK THE CLOUDY DAYS

When you ask people, 'How was your day?' the commonest answer is 'not too bad'. In other words, it could have been a lot worse, but it wasn't that good either.

In weather terms, this equates to a cloudy day with the odd patch of sunshine, but without those cloudy days in our lives it's almost impossible to go from the lows to the highs. It's these dull patches that we often simply take for granted; they are the times that are full of people and things that are so familiar we've almost forgotten them – like the beating of our heart, the air we breathe, the water in the tap, the people who provide for us every day (whether it's parents and partners or the postman and the plumber who look after our needs).

If you don't appreciate what you already have, how can you expect anything else?

LIFT OFF FROM YOUR LOWS

There is nothing more certain than the knowledge that the winds of change will bring disappointment and despair into our lives at times; all of us will have to face periods when it seems that it doesn't just rain but it pours.

But like plants that need both sun and rain to grow, and like the seasons that bring frost and decay to make way for warmth and rebirth, we all are shaped by these highs and lows in our lives.

In fact, many of the happiest people have gone through major pain to get there. And the most successful have had a career that has been riddled with rejections. What sets such people apart is not the number of lows in their lives – it's the way they've learned from them and responded to the situations (remember Mindset on Monday).

We'd all agree that at our lowest points we feel absolutely miserable and often inconsolable, and these episodes may last for days, weeks, months or even years, but the good news is that the only way from our lowest point is up!

Time is a great healer and when the time is right, our pain will be transformed into personal growth.

So, to think positively and to achieve No Regrets on Sunday, remember that those lowest points in our lives are there for three important purposes:

1   They provide us with a contrast. Without lows we cannot truly appreciate the cloudy days or the highs.

2   They provide us with the knowledge that, on reflection, we do have the confidence to manage change and the capabilities to respond to challenges in our lives. We've been there, seen it, done it and felt it before.

3   They might provide us with clues to our future purpose in life. For example, people who have personally experienced relationship breakdowns, loss of a job, antisocial behaviour, drug abuse or cancer are often well placed to offer advice to others. We may even be paid to pursue our purpose. For instance, a mum whose son suffered from a rare eating disorder established her own highly successful nutrition business which now employs over 60 people. Finally, remember that happiness is like the sun: it still goes on shining even though for us it may be cloudy or night time. The real question to ask yourself is, 'Are you blotting out your sun until Friday night – or letting it shine all through the week?'

■ CASE STUDY: Don't let other people diss your ability

John is a social entrepreneur with a passion for sport and disability. After a bout of polio when he was two, he was restricted to callipers and latterly to a wheelchair.

At 14 years old, John was sat down by his school careers adviser and told, 'Don't worry about trying to find a job.

We have jobs set aside for people like you. There are two options. You can be a lift attendant, or if you don't want that, a car park attendant.' This was like a red rag to a bull to John, who dismissed the advice and decided to take control of the situation himself.

Over the next 10 years John developed a portfolio of jobs, but he always retained his passion for empowering individuals with physical disabilities to be all they can be. His vision, from the age of 30, was to create a unique sporting academy which provided an environment for young people to reach their full potential. It was around this time that he dragged me into his rather cluttered office and climbed on to the top of a cupboard to rescue a set of dusty plans which he had drawn up as part of his vision. Blowing off the dust, he excitedly presented a visual layout of what he was dreaming about building. He had basically shown this tatty document to everybody who walked into his life, trying to engage them in his mad idea!

Soon, it became apparent to John that to focus on this dream he couldn't have his mind going off on a tangent and he couldn't get caught up in the rat race of buying bigger houses, paying larger mortgages and having to work in jobs that he hated in order to sustain the lifestyle he had created for himself, only to be too tired to enjoy what he'd got. He therefore decided to move to a smaller house in a cheaper area in order to channel his energies into what really mattered.

Seven years on, the Sports Academy has been built and opened to the public. But John hasn't stopped there; he has gone on to develop an amazing array of creative programmes and services – including wheelchair hockey, which enables both physically able and disabled children to compete on an equal footing. In addition, he has created a number of social enterprises ranging from gardening projects to respite care services.

John has always been true to his vision and has never allowed anybody to shatter his dreams. Even when he was struck by throat cancer he fought it off and is now spending every hour possible writing funding proposals while managing the coffee shop in the Sports Academy.

John is working with us at Windmills to run a no regrets programme for a new generation of young people keen to make their difference in the world in an enterprising way. His belief is that we all suffer from a similar disability – we let other people diss our ability!

'The secret to happiness is not in doing what one likes to do, but in liking what one has to do.'

Anonymous

THINK...

BUILD YOUR OWN RAINBOW

When there's both sun and rain about, the glimpse of a rainbow spanning the sky will lift our spirits.

Of course you'll face showers as well as sunshine throughout your life, but luckily there's a way to build your own rainbow. The secret is to find out what passions and purposes make your life more fulfilling. Once you've established this you can set about filling more of your week with them – whether through your working, learning, playing or giving. You'll soon find the outlook appears so much brighter.

FIND YOUR FULFILMENT FACTOR

Here's a quick challenge that will help you to build a list of all the things you are really interested in, feel strongly about, or that give meaning to your life.

Take a piece of paper and list all the things you are passionate about – your interests, hobbies, sporting activities, community involvement – anything that fires you up. Think about what really gives you purpose and excites you in each area of your life:

1 your working life
2 your learning life
3 your playing life
4 your giving life

Give yourself five minutes to generate as many ideas as possible. Now add to this list by considering the following:

- You have five minutes in a bookshop: which topic sections do you go to first?

- What do you talk about with passion over a pint or a coffee with friends?

- What section of the paper do you read first?

- If you had your time again, what role would you take on?

- What do you look forward to doing at the weekends?

- If you were to go on a quiz programme, what would be your specialist subjects?

- If friends were asked what they think makes you come alive, what would they say?

- What issues get you hot under the collar?

- What work issues do you and your friends/colleagues get passionate about?

- If you could have anybody else's role in life, what sector or field would you be in?

- What purposes or causes matter most to you?

- What new sense of direction or purpose have you gained from your lowest points in life?

- If you won the lottery, what would you spend your time doing, and what purpose or cause would you give back to?

- What would you like to be remembered for?

We all gain fulfilment from different things in life: some come from our passions and interests, others from specific purposes or causes. Add to your list by taking a look at the following A–Z. Highlight all the areas below that give you pleasure, meaning or challenge.

A

Accounting	Acting	Addiction
Advertising	Advocacy	Affliction
Agriculture	Aids	Aircraft
Alcoholism	Alternative therapies	Animals
Antiques	Archaeology	Architecture
Arts	Astrology	Astronomy

B

Babies	Baking	Bands
Banking	Beauty	Bee keeping
Bereavement	Blogging	Boats
Books	Breakdowns	Brewing
Broadcasting	Building	Buying

C

Campaigning	Camping	Cancer
Capitalism	Care	Careers
Cars	Charity	Chess
Children	Cinema	Citizenship
Climate	Coaching	Comedy
Community	Computers	Conflict
Conservation	Construction	Cooking
Counselling	Countries	Creativity
Cricket	Crime	Cruelty
Culture	Cycling	

D

Dancing	Debt	Decorating
Democracy	Design	Diets
Disasters	Discrimination	Disability
Disease	Diving	Divorce
DIY	Documentaries	Drama
Driving	Drugs	

E

Ecology	Economy	Education Elderly
Electronics	Energy	Engineering
Entertainment	Environment	Equality
Ethics	Ethnicity	Events
Extinction		

F

Faith	Family	Famous people
Fashion	Fear	Feminism
Festivals	Films	Fine art
Fish	Fitness	Flowers
Flying	Food	Football
Freedom	Fun	Fundraising
Furniture		

G

Gambling	Games	Gaming
Gangs	Gardening	Gay Issues
Genealogy	Geography	Geology
Gifts	Globalisation	Golf
Gossip	Greed	Gym

H

Hair	Handiwork/crafts	Healing
Health	History	Holidays
Homelessness	Homes	Horses
Horticulture	Hunger	Hygiene

I

Identity	Illiteracy	Illness
Image	Immigration	Inclusion
Information	Interior design	Internet
Investments	Insects	

J

Jewellery	Jobs	Jogging
Joinery	Jokes	Journalism
Journeys	Junk	Justice

K

Karaoke	Karate	Keep fit
Keyboard	Kidnap	Kindness
Kitchens	Knitting	Knowledge

L

Landscaping	Languages	Laughter
Law	Learning	Legislation
Leisure	Liberty	Literature
Loans	Local government	Loneliness
Love		

M

Magic	Maintenance	Make-up
Marketing	Media	Mediation
Medicine	Migration	Military
Modelling	Money	Motherhood
Motor racing	Museums	Music
Musical instruments		

N

Nature	Neighbourhoods	Netball
Networking	New Age	News
Numbers	Numeracy	Nurturing
Nutrition		

O

Obesity	Obituaries	Obsessions
Occupations	Oceans	Offenders
Olympics	Opera	Opinions
Oppression	Organic food	Organising
Orphans	Outdoor pursuits	Outplacement

P

Painting	Patriotism	Peace
People	Performing	Personnel
Pets	Philosophy	Phobias
Photography	Places	Plants
Playing	Poetry	Politics
Population	Poverty	Prayer
Preservation	Psychology	Publishing
Purchasing		

Q

Qualifications	Quality	Quandaries
Questions	Quests	Quibbles
Quiet	Quizzes	

R

Racism	Radio	Reading
Recreation	Recruitment	Recycling
Reflexology	Refugees	Regeneration
Rehabilitation	Relationships	Religion
Resources	Retail	Riding
Rights	Roads	Royalty
Running		

S

Sadness	Safety	Sailing
Schools	Science	Sex
Shopping	Sightseeing	Singing
Society	Space	Spirituality
Sport	Statistics	Stories
Surfing	Sweets	Swimming

T

Talking	Teaching	Telecommunications
Television	Theatre	Time
Tools	Tourism	Toys
Trade	Trafficking	Training
Travel	Transport	

U

Uncertainty	Uncleanliness	Underdogs
Underemployment	Underprivileged	Underwater
Underwear	Underworld	Unemployment
Unfairness	Unions	Universe

V

Vandalism	Vegetarianism	Vehicles
Ventures	Verse	Victim support
Vintage	Violence	Vocabulary
Volunteering	Vulnerable	

W

Walking	War	Waste
Water	Weather	Weddings
Welfare	Wilderness	Wildlife
Wine	Work	World
World affairs	Writing	

X

Xenophobia

Y

Yoga	Youth

Z

Zoos

The exciting thing is that you now have a combined list of all the things that bring happiness and fulfilment into your life. Each provides doors that open up new working, learning, playing or giving opportunities. For example, 'films' is a whole industry you can be employed in, from writing, set design and camera manufacture to corporate sponsorship and catering on the film set. They also

> 'If our ladder is not leaning against the right wall every step we take just gets us to the wrong place faster.'
>
> **Steven Covey**

provide massive opportunities for you to 'give' – from fundraising adverts and documentaries to youth film projects. But before opening these doors, as we learned on Thursday, the most important thing is to prioritise them.

From the whole list you've created, identify seven areas which have the potential to give you the most pleasure, meaning and challenge in the future. Put these in priority order: the first is the one you are drawn to most, the one that you are most enthusiastic about. Now look back at the skills you love using and are good at (see Thursday) and, taking each passion or purpose in turn, try answering the following questions:

WORKING

What jobs or roles would combine my skills, passions and purposes in life?

LEARNING

How could I find out more about the things that bring real happiness and fulfilment into my life, either formally or informally? Who could I learn from?

PLAYING

Where can I just do them for fun? What relevant clubs, societies or interest groups exist in my local area?

GIVING

Who could benefit most from these passions and purposes? How can I make the greatest difference with my unique set of skills? What voluntary opportunities are available locally, regionally, nationally or globally? If nothing exists, do I need to create my own project, activity or charity?

Try to be as creative as possible in combining these elements. If you struggle, think of the most creative and well-connected people you know and ask them for their ideas. As you'll see in the case studies throughout this book and 101 Ways to Have No Regrets on Sunday on page 201, people have done all sorts of things to make changes to their lives. They've combined their enterprise skills with a passion for cooking to set up their own cake-baking business; used a love of diving and people to establish a community-based diving school; learnt Spanish to get into the tourism industry; combined passions for nature, the environment and training with young people.

Remember, you may not immediately be able to earn a living from all the skills that bring you true fulfilment, but you can make a life from them. We all have the potential to learn more, play more or give more in areas we find truly fulfilling. In life, when one door closes, another opens, but it's the corridor of uncertainty between them that causes us the biggest bother. What one brave step can you take today to open an exciting and purposeful new door?

■ CASE STUDY: Reading between the lines

Coleen was an ex-architect who established her own marketing and design company. As the main breadwinner, with two children about to go to university, her bottom line was to run a successful business that would generate enough income to support her top line – the children's future. The bit 'in between' the two lines was a real passion for reading, which had always been squeezed out and left.

Although she was a bit of a cynic about 'self-help' programmes, she offered to do some pro-bono work for one of our partners, somebody we had connected her with. She designed their logo and business cards for a new venture they were embarking on and by giving something with no expectations, Coleen got loads back – with interest.

She was offered a free place on one of their first Community Leaders programmes, and this experience triggered off two ideas in her mind. Firstly, taking time out from the merry-go-round of life made her realise she didn't have any 'me' time to pursue her passion for reading. Every moment of the day was focused on giving to others – whether family, clients or colleagues. Secondly, she found a purposeful channel through which to pursue her passion – a reading charity – helping adults to re-engage with books and poetry, which led her to conduct an information interview with the Director of the charity, who was part of the Community Leaders programme.

By giving herself time and putting herself in a different space, Coleen has been able to rekindle and reconnect with a dormant passion. Coleen has now joined the reading group as a participant and volunteer. She looks forward to every Wednesday night, which has become the highlight of her week. She loves the fact that you can make friends with people who share similar interests without having to know what their role is.

Bitten by the bug, Coleen has enrolled on an intensive facilitator's programme, which will equip her with the tools and techniques to lead her own reading group in the community. She realised, 'what's the point of continually putting off the important things until someday sometime – when the kids are older, when my business is bigger, when I've got more money in the bank, when I'm less busy?'

Reading between the lines in your life, how can you create space and put yourself into new spaces to bring more passion and purpose into your day? Remember: 'some day' is not a day of the week!

> 'Here is a test to find out whether your mission in life is complete. If you're alive, it isn't.'
>
> **Richard Bach**

ACT...

THE £5 CHALLENGE

Life is too short to spend it being miserable. Now is the time to get out of the routine of wishing your week away. Discard old habits and start to learn and use new approaches that will leave you with No Regrets on Sunday.

Countless research shows that one of the greatest influences on happiness and fulfilment is 'giving something back'. So here's your chance to put theory into practice and to engage with one of your passions also.

Your challenge is to 'Make the World a Better Place with £5'. The only rule is that you can't just give the £5 to someone: instead you must take the money and with your own skills and passions, make a difference by making someone 'smile'.

Be enterprising with your £5 and make more of it; be mindful of who and what is around you, and if you can't find a cause in the next hour, keep thinking and be sure to follow up tomorrow. Where is the greatest need in your local community? Who needs cheering up at work? Is there someone who would really appreciate your time? Is there a cause dear to your heart you could make contact with?

Look at your list of the seven areas that have the potential to give you the greatest feeling of fulfilment in your life and make your £5 count towards one of these passions:

Sharing	You need to share your unique combination of skills, passions and experience with someone or something else. The £5 is there to help you on your way.
Meaningful	It will work best when it's something that's meaningful and purposeful to you and the person or cause you are focusing on.
Impact	It needs to 'make a difference', however big or small, to someone else's life. Connect with other people to make a difference greater than you could do by yourself.
Legacy	The impact needs to last. You may wish to keep it going yourself, hand it over to someone else, repeat it or help others to keep it going.
Enjoyable	Make sure it's fun; link it to your passions. Frame the experience as a chance to 'play'.

Please don't make reasonable excuses that you don't have enough time, money or creativity. Jump into this task today. If you need inspiration, here are a few things that over 500 ten-year-olds have done to combine their £5 with their skills and passions:

- Bought a person a bunch of flowers.

- Used the money to buy secondhand instruments and organised a show at a local care home.

- Made a 'bat box' to provide a safe habitat for nesting bats as part of a local conservation project.

- Bought a bucket and sponges and arranged a car wash, then used the £120 raised to buy play equipment for local children with special needs.

- Dug a vegetable plot.

- Designed a cookbook for elderly people.

- Created a photo album for people suffering from Alzheimer's.

- Found sponsorship to buy 400 helium balloons, tying a teabag or seed to each, then asking people to have a cup of tea with a neighbour or plant the seed.

It's up to you to make it happen. You may even want to team up with other people at work, in college or with friends and family. Let us know how you get on – email us on noregrets@windmill-sonline.co.uk and tell us what impact it makes to the person or people at the receiving end of your gesture. Try to make this giving into a habit. You don't have to lay out £5 every time, but you can give away something far more valuable – your time. So how about spending less time unconsciously losing time and instead think about spending it on volunteering?

Great news, you've done brilliantly in your reading, thinking and acting throughout the week so far. Before enjoying the weekend, though, it may be worth having a quick recap of today and the last few days reflecting on what you've learned, what surprises or puzzles you and the difference your actions have made. You may well be left with unanswered questions, conversations you need to have or actions you simply need to pluck up courage or conviction to take.

One small thing may have made all the difference. It could be a change of mindset about a particular issue, more creative use of your time, the development of a new role, uncovering hidden talents, rekindling an old passion or a commitment to a new purpose. Wherever you are at is great: what Saturday will help you do is to pull all your ideas together and create an inspiring and satisfying vision for your future.

FRIDAY: RECAP

- *Be grateful for what is worthwhile in your life and enjoy the simple pleasures that are close to your heart.*

- *Be aware of your levels of happiness and fulfilment and ensure that they reflect on who you are and what you cherish in life, rather than what those around you may feel.*

- *Be imaginative and creative in the way you combine your passions and purposes to build fulfilment into every aspect of your life.*

'We make a living by what we get. We make a life by what we give.'

Winston Churchill

6

SATURDAY
SATISFACTION

There are two really important
dates in your life – the day
you are born, and the
day you understand why

'If you can dream it, you can do it.
Always remember that this thing was
started with a dream and a mouse.'

Walt Disney

READ...

MAKE TIME TO RECHARGE

Saturday traditionally marked the start of the weekend which had a clear demarcation from the working week. Our weekends used to be a space for play, rest and reflection; a time to celebrate the magic moments of the past week and recharge for the coming one. They also provided the opportunity to step back from the everyday chaos and activity and spend time considering questions such as: why am I here? What motivates me? Who matters most to me? What do I consider true contentment?

The weekends give us space to reflect on how happy our lives are, or perhaps consider what we want to change about them. For many, Saturdays are 'play days', when we connect with the things that give us most satisfaction in life. The worrying thing is that this precious time is being gobbled up by the pace of modern life. Saturday is fast becoming an extension of the working week. The constant onslaught of our daily business never slows down. The laptop is switched on, we are playing catch-up with emails, acting as chauffer for the kids, cramming trolleys full of shopping and catching up on all the house-work before we are back to work on Monday – the danger being that we become like a hamster on a wheel, going nowhere fast.

Having the time to pause, think and talk honestly about the things

'Pragmatism does not mean limiting the dream, it means living the dream.'

Julia Hausemann

that are important to us with the people who really matter is a vital aspect of our overall well-being. And providing the opportunity for others to do the same is often the greatest gift we can give.

Whether it's Saturday or some other day, the important thing is to find space in our hectic schedules to pause, reflect and talk. So give yourself time today to step back, look at the bigger picture and ask yourself what you really want from the rest of your life.

TURN YOUR DREAMS INTO REALITY

Just think how brilliant it would be if we could redesign our week to ensure that all our hopes and dreams have come true. The big question is do you know what your hopes and dreams are? It's great if you do, but then do you know how you are going to make them real throughout the rest of your life?

These are such big questions that we usually avoid asking them in the first place and settle for what we believe is a reasonably okay existence – the path of least resistance. The problem with this is that we can then end up living to have regrets only when we reach the end of our life and look back on it.

However, it is exciting to know that we already have all the necessary skills to plan the rest of our life. These are the very same ones we use to plan things like, for example, a holiday. We create a clear vision of where we want to go – whether it's a city break or sunny beach. We know what we want to do when we get there – party, explore the sights or simply chill out. We also know who we want to go with – by ourselves, with the family, or perhaps with a group of friends. We're great at researching the best deals and, most importantly, we know what to pack that's appropriate for the location. The big difference between planning a holiday and planning your life is that, instead of planning for a few weeks or perhaps months, we're planning for a lifetime.

So you have a choice – are you going to abdicate responsibility and rely on the travel agent to book you on to the package tour to hell along with thousands of other tourists floating aimlessly around the world? Or are you going to organise your own trip of a lifetime? This could be a journey based on places you know you'll love, travelling with people you know you'll have fun with, and doing the things that really excite you. The choice is yours.

Imagine looking back in old age and wondering how that trip of a lifetime took such a wrong turn. What could you have done to save yourself from ending up so full of regrets?

SEVEN REASONS WHY OUR WISHES DON'T COME TRUE

1 WE DON'T MAKE WISHES IN THE FIRST PLACE. Without a picture of what we truly want, other people will spray-paint their wishes on to your blank canvas. So take time out to list the top 10 things you'd love to be, do and have over the course of your life. Keep this list handy and look at it every day.

2 WE FAIL TO MAKE SPACE FOR THEM. We fail to prioritise and leave the most important things until we've done what we think is really urgent first. So take your wishes more seriously, schedule them into your diary and don't defer them at any cost.

3 WE SABOTAGE THEM. Imagine two voices, one on each shoulder. The voice on your left plays safe – it is fearful, sticks to

the rules, hates uncertainty and sees change as a danger. It says: 'you can't', 'stay where you are', or 'it's too risky'.

The voice on the right wants you to experiment and take risks – it imagines, explores, likes breaking the rules and is open to anything. It says: 'go for it', 'anything is possible', 'think bigger', 'time to change', or 'why not?' Which voice is shouting loudest at this very moment? When making your wishes initially, turn a deaf ear to that voice on the left – at this early stage it will try to sabotage them. Ways to ignore it include writing down your first thoughts without analysing them, playing music, thinking big, using pictures and being as creative and imaginative as possible.

4 WE'RE NOT CLEAR ENOUGH. All our hopes and dreams are out there waiting for us to catch them and bring them into our life. Have you ever bought a new car and then suddenly started to notice lots of cars around that are the same model and colour? The fact is everything you are looking for is out there, but you're often simply not conscious of it. The clearer you can picture what you want, the quicker you'll get there. If you're crystal clear on what you want and careful what you wish for, you may well get it!

5 WE DON'T TALK ABOUT THEM. The more people that know what you're looking for, the more people there are to keep an eye out for it. Share your hopes with your partner or seek out your fairy godparent – someone who can actually help by encouraging, guiding, inspiring or coaching you towards your goal. Find people who are close to achieving the kind of thing you are hoping for: a colleague who has started their own business, a friend who has changed job to gain a closer match to

what matters to them, or a family member who is learning a new skill, and ask them how they feel your skills and experience can best be used.

6   THEY'RE UNREALISTIC. Dare to dream, but keep your feet firmly on the ground. We've all pondered what we would do if we won the lottery – and we all understand that it's unlikely to happen. So if you always keep a sense of perspective in your dreams, you're less likely to be disappointed if they don't all come to fruition.

7   WE GIVE UP HOPE. We can live about 40 days without food, about three days without water and just a few minutes without air, but it's hard to live for one second without hope. Our wishes can be washed away in an instant by a negative comment, a rejection or a sudden loss of confidence. The solution to this problem is to plan different routes for reaching what you wish for and to create a Plan B (even Plans C, D, E and so on if necessary!) A word of warning: avoid sharing your hopes with negative people – they'll infect you with their cynicism and lack of hope. Most importantly, trust in yourself. After all, if you don't, who will?

Life gives us all our own personal Golden Ticket to no regrets, but it comes to us totally blank. It's up to us to fill in the detail of the journey. Make sure you enjoy every step you take on the way, and remember it's never too late to change direction.

'Whatever you can do or dream you can do, begin it! Boldness has power, magic and genius in it.'

Goethe

■ CASE STUDY: Clearing your runway

The condor is a magical bird that flies gracefully in the sky; however, its carefree flight is threatened by the fact that humans find it a rare delicacy. Due to its large wingspan the condor needs a long clear runway on which to gather speed in order to launch into the air. The way the hunters trap the bird is to go into the thorny shrub and bushland, clear a tiny circle in the middle and lay out the food for the bird on the ground. The condor, flying freely in the sky, swoops down to grab the food only to find that when the hunters arrive it has no clear runway from which to launch and escape.

The same applies to us in our lives. We let stuff happen and grow around us without realising it and soon become trapped and encircled by thorny issues, unable to take control. This was a classic dilemma for Steve, who recently organised his executive team to come on one of our workshops.

Steve was a high-flier, jetting all over the world in a fast-growing nuclear business. His wife and family had forgotten who he was because work had engulfed him. Even when they did have quality time together his phone would ring; it even got to the stage where his wife Gill threatened to throw his BlackBerry® in the ocean while on holiday.

During the programme, Steve sat quietly, trying to make sense of his future; he drew up an amazing Golden Ticket that involved him and his family creating their own business. Before he left that day he proceeded to tell his whole team about his ideas and to his surprise found people wanting to work with him and give practical advice to move forward. Three months later, Steve reviewed his progress with us. The night he left the workshop he went to his wife and excitedly talked her through the idea, to which her response was 'you should have done this years ago'. The next day at work, for the first time ever, he received a text from her saying how excited she was about their talk and the opportunities ahead. He then phoned his rather sceptical 18-year-old son to pass the idea by him, thinking this would be the acid test – a more critical and realistic view. He was taken aback by his son's really positive response. Finally, he emailed his daughter with a job specification for a marketing assistant in a new, fast-growing consultancy business. She immediately and excitedly rang her mum up saying, 'Somebody wants to offer me a job,' to which her mum said, 'That's your dad's new business.'

That weekend the company was registered and the whole family had their first board meeting, at which Steve's son designed their new logo and they all discussed how this new venture could move forward. Steve's decision was not a black and white one; it wasn't about jumping out of his current high-flying plane and setting up his own glider; his plan had to be more considered than that. He was to slowly reduce his hours within his current role, while retaining a steady income, but at the same time become an interim consultant for their developing business, using his extensive network of friends and colleagues as potential new clients.

Steve understood how important it is to engage all the people you care about in the process. The exciting thing for Steve is that in setting up his family business he is not only potentially spending more time with his family but is also helping them to live their dreams.

THINK...

YOUR GOLDEN TICKET

This creative exercise is one of the most exciting things you can do. It helps you create and live out your own Golden Ticket to the future. It draws together the ideas and actions you have considered as you have travelled throughout the week so far; it builds on the positive mindset you've created; blends your working, learning, playing and giving; brings your ideal roles to life; boosts the talents you love; and begins with fun in mind. This exercise will be complemented by Sunday, too, when we look at the people who support you to achieve your hopes and dreams.

READY – Check you are prepared for the journey ahead:

- Don't leave your packing to the last minute. Give yourself the time and space this exercise deserves.

- Throw out any negative baggage – remember that you are a special person and you've achieved an amazing amount so far in your life.

- Fly high – don't limit yourself, get that helicopter view and remember that anything is possible.

STEADY – Get a blank piece of paper and write 'My Golden Ticket' at the top. Now pick a date in the future – it could be six months, a year, five, ten or twenty years ahead. Make it far enough away for you to be creative, but also close enough to be of relevance. Five years ahead may be a good option. Write this date on the top right-hand corner of your Golden Ticket.

GO – For the rest of this exercise, imagine it is now that date in the future. You've travelled in a time capsule to your future and you've had the most extraordinary and amazing journey of your life so far. All your hopes and dreams have come true and you have absolutely no regrets.

Now write down on your Golden Ticket your answers to the following questions. Don't stop to analyse your thoughts – just go with the flow and be as big, bold and imaginative as you can. Use sketches, symbols, doodles or anything else that helps you visualise your future.

WORKING

YOU'RE IN YOUR IDEAL JOB, WHAT IS IT?

- What are you doing?
- Who are you working for?
- Where are you working?
- Are you in part- or full-time employment?
- Are you self-employed or an employee?

WHAT DOES YOUR AVERAGE WORKING WEEK LOOK LIKE?

- Where are you based?
- Who are you working with?
- How long is your working day?
- You're now using the skills you love – how are you doing this, and for what purpose?
- You're passionate about your work – why?
- In what way is your new job really purposeful?

WHY ARE YOU NOW PROUD OF YOUR WORK?

- What have been the most fun and fulfilling moments?
- List all your major achievements, projects and experiences over the past few years. What impact have you personally made?

LEARNING

YOU'VE GROWN AS A PERSON – BUT HOW?

- What formal and informal learning have you undertaken?
- What mentors have you learned from?
- What learning opportunities have you created – courses, qualifications, secondments?

YOU'RE MORE EMPLOYABLE NOW, WHY?

- What new skills, knowledge and experience have you gained?
- How are you combining your talents and passions in a fun way?
- What speciality or expertise have you developed?
- What are you best known for?

WHERE HAVE YOU TAKEN RISKS?

- In which aspects of your life have you taken a real leap of faith?
- How have you grown in confidence and stretched your comfort zone?
- With the knowledge that you couldn't fail, what brave step did you take?

PLAYING

FUN FILLS EVERY DAY, IN WHICH WAY?

- You've had the most enjoyable years of your life, what have you been up to?

- How have you rekindled all your old passions, interests and hobbies?

- You've been in places and with people that make you come alive – where have you been?

YOU'RE PLAYING YOUR PART– BUT HOW?

- Which of the roles you are currently playing is the most fun and fulfilling?

- Your personal well-being is brilliant physically, mentally and emotionally – why?

YOUR SOCIAL LIFE IS EXCELLENT – WHY?

- Who have you spent quality time with? What have you enjoyed doing with friends or as a family?

- Which old friends have you got back in touch with? What new relationships have you developed?

GIVING

HOW HAVE YOU MADE A REAL DIFFERENCE?

- You've given your time and talents to people you love – family, friends, colleagues, community. Who have you given to and what have you given them?

- You've supported purposes you're passionate about – in what way?

YOU'VE LEFT YOUR LEGACY, WHERE?

- Where have you left a lasting mark?

- If you passed away this day, what would you like to be remembered for?

- Who have you worked with to make a bigger difference?

YOU'VE ABSOLUTELY NO REGRETS – WHY?

- Why is it you're so fulfilled and content with the life you now have?

■ CASE STUDY: The richest person in the graveyard

Kenny never worked, couldn't read or write, slept on an old couch and didn't have a penny. His only possessions were a couple of dirty sets of clothes, a Liverpool scarf, which never left his neck, and three teeth! Yet Kenny was the richest person I've ever met.

I've been privileged enough to spend quality time in two very different locations: one where footballers live and which is financially rich but emotionally poor, and another, which is financially poor yet emotionally rich.

As a volunteer at the Thursday Club, a social club for adults with learning difficulties in the heart of Toxteth, I've been lucky enough to have been friends with Kenny for over 23 years. He never missed a club night, and he was always there before everyone else to set up the snooker table, disco and arts equipment. He

'Luck is a matter of preparation meeting opportunity.'

Oprah Winfrey

had both the strongest smell and the strongest hug, always put his hand up to push the wheelchairs, organised the rounders match and whenever he was given any money he immediately spent it on presents for the kids.

Kenny was a human being not a human doing. He had no money, but he was extremely rich.

Over a period of time Kenny complained of a bad stomach, but doctors put it down to a poor diet. Tragically, in his late forties Kenny passed away with cancer. The sad thing was that he could have been operated on if he had been a fitter, healthier person.

Kenny's funeral was the best-attended service I've ever seen. It gave me a chance to really stop and consider the two distinct attitudes to personal wealth. Some people focus on acquiring shares, others simply share. Some are obsessed by rates of interest, others rate genuine interest. Some see happiness in terms of financial balance, others as a work/life balance. Some people live for their savings, others save people's lives! Kenny never dreamed of having wealth or doing a high-powered job. He was happy being who he was.

Are you a have, do, be person, where financial richness and material wealth are king? Or are you a be, do, have person, where being at ease with yourself and giving to others are the most precious things? How 'rich' is your Golden Ticket? What do the words share, interest, balance and saving mean to you?

Finally, review the ideas you've created and add anything else, however big or small, to your Golden Ticket. What else in the world would you love to give to, and what would you like to receive from it?

Now imagine you have reached this future point with absolutely no regrets. You've achieved everything on your Golden Ticket and more. Looking back at the journey you've taken to achieve your Golden Ticket, answer the questions below, completing each sentence:

- IN ACHIEVING ALL MY GOALS, THE BIGGEST OBSTACLE I OVERCAME WAS ... (Write down the most daunting obstacle you faced.)

- I OVERCAME THIS BY ... (You didn't give up, blame something or someone else. You took responsibility. What did you do?)

- THE PEOPLE WHO HELPED ME WERE ... (We all need people to support us, so who made the greatest difference? Who was the first positive person you shared your Golden Ticket with? Or maybe even created one with?)

- THE FIRST BRAVE STEP I TOOK WAS ... (Every journey starts with a first step. What did you do to begin to make it real? And remember the first step may be in your head!)

- I KEPT ON GOING BY ... (Many of us start out full of enthusiasm but can forget our destination, get sidetracked by other people or simply let life grind us down. How did you keep the momentum going?)

Congratulations, you've now created an inspiring Golden Ticket to your future and have identified the first step to make it real. If you don't feel inspired by it or if it seems too great a task to begin, try the exercise again or work on a small part of it that really excites you. The more times you do this, the bolder and more creative you will become.

Don't worry if your Golden Ticket isn't crystal clear. When asked once what his vision of the future was, Walt Disney replied, 'All I know is it's fun, colourful and glitzy.' The rest, as they say, is history.

'Destiny is not a matter of chance. It is a matter of choice. It is not something to be waited for. It is something to be achieved.'

William Jennings Bryan

So focus on the bits of your Golden Ticket that jump out as the most exciting and meaningful to you, and be open to all the new possibilities along the way. Keep thinking about how great you'll feel when you've achieved the best bits of your Golden Ticket, but be prepared to keep everything real.

Make it real today, within the next hour, by doing something really simple and practical to live out part of your Golden Ticket. Why wait days to live your dreams when you can dream up ways of living them today?

We all have loads of imagination, so use yours the right way – to create the dreams that will make your life worthwhile.

Here are five simple steps to make your Golden Ticket a reality:

1 Write down all your ideas
2 Believe you can achieve
3 Focus on the benefits
4 Plan small realistic steps
5 Finally, tell as many people as possible what you're planning

Make the most of it and enjoy the journey of a lifetime.

■ CASE STUDY: Pressing the right button

The simple difference between dreams and nightmares, worry and hope, fear and optimism, is the way in which we choose to use our imagination. We are all given the gift of imagination, but we are also given the choice of how we use it – positively or negatively.

James had chosen a positive approach, in order to create and realise three Golden Tickets by his early forties. They grew, a bit like Russian dolls, with the same core values but involved a progressively bigger vision. James was privileged enough to be able to establish a groundbreaking unit which created jobs and economic wealth in an under-developed region. The unit was based in a traditional educational institution and grew to a team of over 20 staff.

James was a bit of a maverick and so he never quite fitted within a hierarchical and bureaucratic organisation. With the appointment of a new leader, the institution undertook a major restructuring and the unit was then deemed to be surplus to requirements. It was at 9pm one February evening that James received a phone call at home from the HR director, explaining the news. Although James knew changes were on the way, he never realised how severe they would be. In one phone call his bubble had burst. His Golden Ticket had just been ripped to pieces.

Faced with a situation that seemed to be totally out of his control, James sat at the bottom of the stairs with his head in his hands. His mind switched immediately to a nightmare situation – unemployed and therefore unable to pay the mortgage and support his young family, and plunged into a situation of complete uncertainty. Everything seemed to be in pieces; in an instant James had subconsciously chosen to create that negative domino effect in his head – panic, anxiety, depression, no hope, no home and no future! He had jumped on to the downward escalator heading rapidly for the depths of despair. After a little while James dragged himself upstairs and broke the news to his wife Michelle, who was watching TV in bed, unaware of the phone call. Her immediate response was totally different: 'This is your chance to go it alone and not be held back. You've done it before so why can't you now? This is a brilliant opportunity.' Things suddenly felt different. While James couldn't control the situation, he could control how he thought about it. He could press the panic button and zoom rapidly down the escalator, ending up trapped in a dark place, or choose to take the lift upwards, accepting the situation and realising he had more control, which would enable him to be braver. Most importantly, he realised that he had positive people around him.

Over the next six months, James partnered with an ex-colleague he trusted and valued enormously to establish their own new business and charity.

James, like many of us, could have easily carried on pressing the wrong button, but he had a choice and this was made far easier with the support of his wife Michelle, who hit the right button for him. There is no doubt that you will have a choice in the way you use your imagination in the future. Whatever happens, are you going to let your Golden Ticket fall to pieces, or are you going to lift off, rise above all the challenges and reach peace? It's your choice which button you press!

ACT...

If you don't have a dream, you can never make your dream come true. The trouble is, we often fail to create a clear, detailed picture of what we want from life.

SEND YOURSELF A POSTCARD

As I've said, people spend more time planning their two weeks' holiday than the other 50 weeks of their year. So today's task is not only to plan for your trip of a lifetime, but to reach the first destination within 24 hours.

1 Explore the Golden Ticket you have just made and highlight the elements that:

  - Excite you so much that they really jump out at you and draw you towards them

  - Have the potential to create a positive ripple effect on other dimensions of your Golden Ticket

  - Can be easily made real with a couple of brave steps

2 Pick one element that fits all three criteria and you feel motivated enough to do something about.

3 See this as a 'destination' on your trip towards no regrets.

4   Imagine you have to take a brave step to get to this destination within the next 24 hours. What would this brave step be? Where would it take you?

Buy a postcard and write yourself a note that you need to be reminded of in 24 hours' time. On the postcard imagine you are at this new destination, and include:

- Where you are now;

- What it looks and feels like;

- What are the best bits of this new place;

- What your first brave step was to get you here;

- Where you are going and what are you going to do next.

5   Now address the postcard to yourself and post it in the nearest postbox. Your goal is to achieve your first brave step before the postcard arrives home.

6   Over time you could repeat the exercise. You may wish to send the postcard to a friend, asking them to send it back to you at a later date. Perhaps make a pledge to send yourself a postcard once a week so that you ensure that you regularly make progress towards your Golden Ticket.

The good news is you are not alone in your journey; achieving No Regrets on Sunday is made easier with the support of others; we all need friends to encourage us along the way. Moving on to tomorrow, Sunday will help you explore the key relationships that are important to making your Golden Ticket a reality. First, remind yourself of the key points from today.

SATURDAY: RECAP

- *Make sure you step back, look at the bigger picture and create your own Golden Ticket.*

- *Focus on the aspects of the vision you have created that excite and inspire you the most. These will be the things that will really motivate and energise you to make it real.*

- *Create an early win. Do something practical that turns your thinking and ideas into action.*

'If you don't know where you are going, you'll end up somewhere else.'

Yogi Berra

7

SUNDAY
SUPPORT

Want to change someone else's
life? Why not start with your own?

'I keep six honest serving men,
they taught me all I knew:
Their names are What and Why and When
and How and Where and Who.'

Rudyard Kipling

READ...

REMEMBER THE PEOPLE WHO REALLY COUNT

Sunday is the last day in this process to having no regrets; it's a time to reflect on how far you have travelled over the last week and who you have been travelling with. As you will have learned by now, taking control of your life is not only dependent on taking personal responsibility but also about our personal relationships with other people. Today is a chance to explore how the right support will help you attain and maintain your hopes and dreams.

From your Golden Ticket and the other actions you have taken part in throughout the week you may have lots of exciting ideas for the future – ideas that you know will leave you with no regrets when you look back on your life. However, to make these ideas a reality you need to keep working at them, and sometimes you need a helping hand to keep yourself on the right track.

Our experience shows that, even with the best intentions, only 5 to 10 per cent of people have the drive to take control of their lives on their own and keep the momentum going. The fact is that all of us need support to overcome obstacles and reach our goals – and we find it comes from different groups of people.

This support tends to begin at the very start of life. At birth we're greeted by the midwife and a team of medical specialists who will see us safely through the first week, and as we go through childhood, people feed us, pass on their values and watch over us. As we begin to learn, we gain advice, guidance, encouragement and support from teachers, coaches and peers. When as adults we enter the working world, we get support from employers, colleagues, mentors and role models.

Day by day, different people appear to help us along the way. When we face change or transition, there are people around us to provide comfort, advice, information and contacts. Right from the time you were a child in the playground there have been people, who were there for you – people who matter most and play the biggest part in your daily life. The sooner we recognise the value of support from others, the more improved are our chances of making our wishes come true. It is important to remember that if we feel that we lack support, we should never be afraid to ask for help.

> 'To the world you may be one person, but to one person you may be the world.'
>
> **Unknown**

When life's challenges knock us off course, friends give us emotional support, but throughout our daily routine there are all sorts of 'invisible people' who keep us happy, comfortable and secure – from the train driver who gets us to work to the person stacking the supermarket shelves, or the street sweeper.

Most important of all, right through our lives we know we can rely on our nearest and dearest to simply love us for who we are. When we look back on the Sunday evening of our life, our qualifications, status and possessions will evaporate into thin air; what will remain and endure is the value of all those people who've been there for us.

WHO SITS ON YOUR BENCH?

Remember the playground and all the exciting possibilities it held for you as a child? There were swings, roundabouts, seesaws and slides – all sorts of fun and fulfilment combined with challenges, fears, bumps and bruises.

Life itself is just like that – you face all kinds of ups and downs, balancing acts and obstacles, and often go round in circles, but there's one simple object that is often overlooked in the playground – the bench – and it's one of the most important of all of them.

That bench is deliberately placed to give watchful parents and carers a good view of the whole playground and is often surrounded by such helpful things as prams, toys, packed lunches and bikes. It provides a resting place for those who care deeply for us. So who sits on your bench? Who is ready to jump up and encourage you when you're stuck? Pick you up when you fall, hug you when you cry or guide you when you are lost?

In the future, who will help you when you fall off the swing, get bumped off the seesaw or spin off the roundabout?

To help you find the answer, take a minute or two to think about the following questions:

- Who are the people who've made the greatest difference in your life to date?

- Why have they made such an impact?

- How have they influenced your purpose?

- Have you thanked them?

- Who else do you need on your bench to fulfil your potential?

- What relationships (new or old) do you need to develop further?

It would be reassuring if every time you faced a challenging situation you could rely on somebody to join you on your bench and offer some helpful advice. Although it's actually quite likely that this is happening to you anyway! Is there somebody challenging your mindset and supporting you in the roles you play? Or perhaps helping you to blend your WLPG and enabling you to lead a more fulfilling life?

Sometimes all you need is someone to value you, your skills and your talents: someone who is prepared to work with you to create an inspiring vision for your future.

WHOSE BENCH ARE YOU SITTING ON?

Everyone needs a little help from their friends – there are six billion other people out there in the world, and most of these have their own bench of supporters. There are also links between all of us – in the special care baby unit, for instance, the baby needs the consultant to survive, the consultant relies on the nurse, the nurse on the nursing support and so on. But all of them would be out of a job without the baby!

Our parents devote their lives to caring for us as children and, hopefully, in return we care for them as they grow old.

We may depend on people from the other side of the

> 'You have not lived a perfect day, unless you have done something for someone who will never be able to repay you.'
>
> **Ruth Smeltzer**

world for our clothes, call centres and football teams, and they in turn provide wealth and happiness for their families and communities. The danger, though, in our consumer society, is that we let our egos swallow up everything around us. We may become so self-centred we lose touch with other people.

To play our part and make the world a better place, we all need to reconnect with what really matters to us. And this means sitting on other people's benches from time to time – whether it's with your family, your friends, your colleagues, your neighbours or simply those people who need your help.

What you give you will get back with interest.

■ CASE STUDY: Taking the plunge together

Richard was in the middle of his working week, and stuck in the middle of the biggest rut of his life. He felt underemployed, undervalued, uninspired and unmotivated. This was compounded by a major restructuring going on in his company which sidelined his role even more.

As part of a cost-cutting exercise, Richard was able to consider whether or not to apply for voluntary severance, and as part of the deal an attractive redundancy deal was put on the table – offering two and a half times his annual salary!

In the ensuing weeks Richard must have run round the playground of life 101 times. He swung from highs to lows each day, spent a lot of time going on the roundabout in circles, kept on seeing the obstacles to overcome on the climbing frame, continually see-sawed over whether to stay or go, and couldn't consider taking the final plunge.

Our team at Windmills spent a number of hours listening, reflecting and gently challenging Richard to try to help him focus. We were very conscious that all sorts of characters had freely offered their views, but without really putting themselves in his shoes. It was important for Richard to make up his own mind, as his decision would have a major ripple effect on those close to him.

The clock was ticking, and even though he gained a few days' extension Richard still couldn't resolve the argument in his head. As the provider for and guardian of his family he felt a self-keeping voice shouting at him: 'Don't risk it, play safe, stay where you are.' He could hear another voice as well, though, and this explorative voice was saying: 'Go for it, you won't get this chance again.'

Richard prepared two letters to his employer – one to stay and one to go – but he still didn't know which one to sign!

At the end of a real rollercoaster of a ride, he was at his wits' end. Until this point he hadn't talked to his children about the dilemma, so on the Friday evening before Monday's deadline, Richard and his wife Deirdre cooked a family meal and asked their 10- and 14-year-olds one simple question: 'Do you think Daddy is happy at work?' The children instantly replied: 'No.' Richard asked them why they thought that and they said, 'You used to come home talking with excitement about your work, showing us what you've done. You stopped that over a year ago, now we see an unhappy face.'

In an instant the decision was made and they agreed to take the plunge together, whatever the consequences.

With the benefit of hindsight, Richard was flabbergasted at how much he had focused on the wrong things, placing too great an emphasis on wealth and materialism at the expense of well-being and the happiness of his children. He also realised how important the little people are on your bench.

THINK...

BUILDING BACK-UP ON YOUR BENCH

Imagine we all have a bench in the playground where people come and go throughout our lives, looking after us through the ups and downs. In this exercise five invisible friends will help you realise your Golden Ticket by building back-up on your bench. Their names are WHY, WHO, HOW, WHERE and WHAT.

STEP 1 – WHY DO I NEED SUPPORT?

Looking at the most exciting elements of your Golden Ticket, think about the opportunities and obstacles to making this real. Be clear about the type of support you need to overcome the obstacles and maximise the opportunities. Try to be as specific as possible as to what sort of help you are looking for. Write a list of all the types of support you need. These may relate to particular days of the week, for example you may need people who can:

- Help you be more positive in your mindset, boost your confidence and belief that you can really achieve it

- Enable you to be more creative and imaginative in blending your working, learning, playing and giving to make your Golden Ticket real

- Encourage you to invest the right time and energy in the roles that really matter and will make the greatest difference

- Explore the skills you love using most and ensure you maximise them

- Inspire you to go beyond your dreams and be a role model for you

- Celebrate your progress and review whether it is taking you in the right direction

STEP 2 – WHO CAN HELP ME?

To help you out, below are a number of different families of characters in the playground of life, each offering different types of support. With the type of support you need in mind, read through their traits and think about how they might be a useful person for you to have on your bench.

- **SAFEKEEPERS** – Always around and looking out for you, their primary role is to keep you safe – to stop you falling, becoming hurt or getting into trouble. They avoid change, uncertainty and risk and always think logically about potential consequences and plan for practical realities.

- **EXPLORERS** – Constantly encouraging you to try new experiences; anything is possible with explorers. It's all about that leap of faith. If you don't do it, who will?

- **CARERS** – When we fall from great heights, get knocked around, hurt by others or feel fragile and sick, the carers give us a big hug, wipe away the tears and bring warmth and reassurance. In a loving and understanding way they are great at making us feel better.

- **DEVELOPERS** – Developers focus on taking us out of our comfort zone, rather than giving us comfort. Instead of dwelling on our knocks and troubles, they motivate us to raise our aspirations, look forward and set new goals that will stretch us. For developers there is no gain without pain.

- **CONNECTORS** – These people sit on the bench and love gossiping – they know everybody and everything that's going on around them. If they can't help out they know somebody who can. Connectors are often extrovert with good interpersonal skills; they are great networkers and excellent at making links between people and understanding the power and the politics.

- **INVISIBLE PEOPLE** – These people play vital roles but we often never see them, so they tend to be taken for granted – the health and safety officer who checks the playground equipment, the manufacturer who made it, the gardener who mows the lawns or the park keeper who collects the litter. We all need to be conscious and thankful of the 'invisible people' who support our daily routine and maintain quality in our lives.

- **BRIGHT SPARKS** – Bright sparks are great at generating new ideas, providing fresh perspectives and creating novel ways for doing things. They have great imagination and are the people who turn climbing frames into spaceships and roundabouts into magical mystery tours. They are great to have around when you need to think outside the box.

- **WISE OWLS** – Wise owls have usually experienced many highs and lows, know what it's like to overcome obstacles and can help you to regulate your speed on the roundabout of life. Like youngsters who have their grandparents to look after them in the playground, we all need to draw on the wisdom and experience of people who have been through similar challenges.

- **BULLIES** – Bullying, whether physical, emotional or financial, is unwelcome and unacceptable in any playground, but from time to time some of us may need someone to nag and cajole us into action. Injecting a bit of tension into our lives can sometimes act as a catalyst for a change of direction.

- **PLAYMATES** – Most of us see belonging to a group or tribe as important to our social lives. We all need friendships, people to share fun and interests with, as well as exchange skills. We need people in work and play who we get on with and ones who'll bring a smile to our faces when we're down.

> 'The key is to keep company only with people who uplift you, whose presence calls forth your best.'
>
> **Epictetus**

■ CASE STUDY: When the tree became the bench

Leslie was in her fifties and throughout her career she had grown from a small acorn to a wise old tree in a global telecommunications company. Her career had branched out in a number of directions, with seasons of colour as well as bare, hard times. Her focus was to climb as high as she could but as a result she lost sight of her true roots – her family and friends.

She had tirelessly but successfully grown to the dizzy heights of Director for European Operations, then one dramatic day the corporate axe came along – the powers that be had decided to restructure and any non-essential resources were to be pruned away.

Uprooted, unemployed and riddled with health problems, Leslie came to Windmills for help, attending one of our programmes. Like any fallen tree, Leslie's solid experience could have been used in a number of ways. She could replant herself in a more fertile environment, lie there and retire gracefully, or literally let herself be broken down into pieces and become a giant bundle of toothpicks.

The programme allowed Leslie to look at her roots for the first time. Her real foundations were her family, particularly her two children; they had complex needs and she had spent many years battling with educational and social services to gain the best support for them. What Leslie discovered was that her core values and her true value to society lay in helping other families get the very best for their children in need.

Since then, Leslie has established a Parent Advocacy Charity which helps people across her city. She has turned from a tree into a bench, helping to support hundreds of families by speaking on their behalf as well as empowering them to stand up for their rights.

Leslie refused to lie down and rot; instead she used the axe to get rid of the dead wood in her life and sculpted her own future. Thirteen years after coming on the programme, Leslie still runs the charity, even though, by her own admission, she is becoming a bit rickety and is in need of a bit of repair!

STEP 3 – HOW CAN THEY HELP ME?

Every character will have a different perspective on the opportunities and problems, and different ideas about how to move forward – they may even take you in unexpected directions.

Bearing in mind your overall priorities, use the checklist opposite to tick how the characters can specifically help you create the most momentum for your Golden Ticket. Think carefully about what specific type of support will create the 'tipping point' to make your vision real.

SAFEKEEPERS	☐ Security	☐ Realism	☐ Planning
EXPLORERS	☐ Courage	☐ Confidence	☐ Possibility
CARERS	☐ Love	☐ Understanding	☐ Reassurance
DEVELOPERS	☐ Motivation	☐ Coaching	☐ Growth
CONNECTORS	☐ Contacts	☐ Knowledge	☐ Specific help
INVISIBLE PEOPLE	☐ Survival	☐ Support	☐ Sustainability
BRIGHT SPARKS	☐ Creativity	☐ Freshness	☐ Energy
WISE OWLS	☐ Guidance	☐ Experience	☐ Perspective
BULLIES	☐ Challenge	☐ Nagging	☐ Pressure
PLAYMATES	☐ Fun	☐ Friendship	☐ Teamwork

Remember that this list is certainly not exhaustive and you may well recognise other characters from your own playground.

The help you need will change frequently too, so it might be an idea to keep this list to hand as you progress towards your goal to help you overcome any obstacles you might meet on the way.

STEP 4 – WHERE WILL I FIND THE RIGHT SUPPORT?

Having ticked the type of help you need, make a list of all the people you know who are best placed to provide it. Then add anybody else who could possibly help (spread your net as wide as possible). It is acknowledged that we are only ever six connections away from a specific person in the world. If you need help, which of these people would be able to provide it, or know someone who could?

The following prompts may help you if you get stuck. Map out everybody you know under the following headings.

WORKING

- PRESENT COLLEAGUES: team, division, organisation
- PAST COLLEAGUES: including former boss(es)
- PEOPLE IN YOUR SECTOR: competitors, clients, etc.

LEARNING

- PRESENT AND PAST CLASSMATES: school or college friends, people you've met on courses
- PROFESSIONALS: teachers, trainers, lecturers
- MENTORS/ROLE MODELS: people who inspire you

PLAYING

- FRIENDS: the address book
- FRIENDS OF FRIENDS: asking people who they know
- SOCIAL CONTACTS: people you've met at parties, etc.

GIVING

- FAMILY
- NEIGHBOURS
- THE WIDER COMMUNITY: people you come into contact with each day

Use your contacts across your working, learning, playing and giving to map out a hit list. For example, an old boss may be able to give you some contacts, your friends' dads may know someone you can talk to, or a former classmate may be in your ideal job. Now prioritise the list. Highlight two or three people that can make the biggest difference. If you're struggling, it's always good to include a 'connector' person who knows everybody.

STEP 5 – WHAT ELSE CAN I DO?
It's always good to create alternatives.

a) Try combining characters
    Remember that each character will have a different perspective on each challenge and possibility you face. One character is no better or worse than another, but it's the way you combine them that counts – you need to bring in the right support at the right time. The Explorers and Developers will encourage you to go beyond and go for it, while the Safekeepers will tell you not to take risks. The Bright Sparks will ask 'have you thought about …?', while the Connectors will suggest people you could speak to. Meanwhile, the Carers will tell you that everything's going to be okay, while the bullies will warn you that you'll be in trouble if you don't act a certain way. For example, if you were considering setting up your own business, there would be little point talking to your father first if he'd always been in a job for life and had never taken risks (a Safekeeper). But having spoken to role models who had already set up their own business (Wise Owls) and gained confidence and contacts (from the Developers and Connectors), it could be worth speaking to your dad about plans to lower the risk. The broader the range of characters

on your bench, the more creatively you can combine them for each new challenge and possibility.

b) Ask yourself for help

Imagine each of the 10 playground characters is always on call, ready to step forward whenever you have a problem to solve or possibility to explore. Imagine your conversation with each of them and then use your intuition or logic (whichever feels right) to choose the best course of action. When you master this creative habit, you'll bring out particular characters for particular situations. If you think this sounds crazy, just remind yourself of all those conversations going on in your head before important meetings, after nights out or during massive arguments!

c) Leaving a legacy

Imagine in 100 years' time there is a plaque on a bench in your favourite beauty spot that celebrates your life. What would be written on it? What would you be remembered for? The size of your house, the speed of your car, or the people's lives you have touched? Think carefully about what talents and qualities you have to offer the world, who needs your help most and when it's time to move on to a new bench. Try not to spread yourself too thinly. Focus your energy on where you can make most difference, but have fun at the same time. Take the plunge today to build back-up on your bench. And,

> 'I've learned that people will forget what you said, people will forget what you did, but people will never forget how you made them feel.'
>
> **Maya Angelou**

more importantly, commit yourself to support one person who needs your help – in the playground of life they may be struggling to keep their balance, stuck on an obstacle, or simply going round in circles!

■ CASE STUDY: Wish you were here!

Sophie was a client of ours at Windmills. A focused and high-powered individual, she was a formidable lady at the best of times. In her forties, she was well known on the conference circuit as a specialist in employability.

However, it was when travelling home from a conference in Bristol that an incident happened that would change her perspective on life. She was tired after her speech and once on the train she took off her shoes and put her feet up on the seat opposite her, only to be confronted by an irate passenger who was outraged that she dared put her feet beside her. Sophie's assertive nature meant she wouldn't compromise, so she ignored the request to remove her feet and fell asleep.

Sophie woke up after an hour to find that not only had the lady opposite her left the train but that her shoes had disappeared too! Having got the whole carriage up looking for them, Sophie then realised that the lady had stolen them.

The next day at a project meeting Sophie angrily related this story to myself and a colleague. Knowing what she was like, we calmly empathised with her and said nothing. On the way back home, though, a cunning plan came into my head. I bought a postcard, wrote a note to Sophie from the pair of shoes and sent it anonymously from a difference postal area. I then phoned up another colleague who sent a second postcard while he was away for the weekend. Within a matter of weeks, unbeknown to Sophie, we had created a script team as big as that of *Coronation Street* and she had received tens of postcards from around the world.

The story developed over time, and the pair of shoes (which we called 'Clever Clogs') went on to marry a pair of loafers, eloping to Australia where they reared a family of flip-flops. A dramatic twist in the story ensued six months later when Clever Clogs was captured and taken hostage by a pair of dirty old boots. As more and more people found out about the story the script team commissioned postcards from every part of the world as people went on their annual holidays. When Sophie retired a number of years later, she had received literally hundreds of postcards, and at her retirement party she was presented with a new pair of slippers!

To this day she doesn't know who sent all the postcards, but what she does know is that the people around her are the things she misses most in retirement – much more than the work itself. She had taken many of these people for granted until they weren't there, but now she makes a conscious effort to keep in touch with the people that matter by doing voluntary and freelance work.

So who will always be there to send you a postcard?

ACT...

THANK YOU

Your life wouldn't be what it is today without the help and support of all the people on your bench. But do you truly appreciate all they've done for you, and, more importantly, have you recently told them how much you value them? Today's task is to do just that.

1   Think of the 10 people who have made the greatest impact on your life so far. They may be family members, friends, partners, colleagues, teachers or role models. They may have played a variety of different roles on your bench.

2   Pick out the one person you would like to really thank today. They may be someone who has made a fundamental difference to your life, or perhaps someone who is always there for you but that you've always taken for granted.

3   Buy a thank-you card and write a letter. Say whatever is important to you and don't hold yourself back. Here are a few things you might want to include:

   •   Thanking them for a specific thing they have done or have provided in your life

   •   Mentioning the qualities you love about them

- Talking about the impact and benefit of their input in your life

- Saying how you feel and what you think about their support

- Looking positively to your relationship in the future

If you don't have a card, just write a letter or send an email.

4   Better still, be brave enough to pick up the phone and actually speak to them in person, now. Prepare, or even read out a prepared script, and don't let them interrupt you. The first time you do this you may feel a bit uncomfortable, but if you make it into a conscious habit you'll become more confident.

5   When you've done this, make your move to add someone else to your list of contacts that one day you would like to thank for their support for helping you achieve your dreams. Look at the two or three people you have prioritised as being most likely to be able to sit on your bench. There's no better time than the present to make a move. Pick up the phone or send a quick email now before your safekeeping self stops you. Start with someone you know, like and respect. Put some time in the diary over the week ahead to build back-up on your bench.

It may seem strange at first, but once you get into the habit, all sorts of wonderful possibilities will emerge. Like plunging down the slide, it's scary at first, but you'll be so glad you did it. Take that plunge today and you'll be amazed where it leads you.

'You have been given a gift of 86,400 seconds today. Have you used one to say "thank you"?'

William A. Ward

Congratulations on reaching the end of your week. This is only the beginning, Monday morning is fast approaching and with it comes all sorts of new possibilities. One new thought, conversation or action may have made all the difference over the last week – it may have even triggered off other ideas and opportunities. What's important now is that you keep this new-found momentum going. The next and final chapter, No Regrets for Life, will help you develop this as a habit of a lifetime.

SUNDAY: RECAP

- *Think about who is on your bench, and why, and consider what changes you may need to make to build further back-up.*

- *Make sure you have different personalities supporting you in different areas of your life – combining characters will provide you with different views on your life and goals.*

- *Remember to thank those who support you, and support others.*

'Alone we can do so little. Together we can do so much.'

Helen Keller

8

NO REGRETS FOR LIFE

You may not be there yet, but you are closer than you were last week

'Any true lasting change comes from inside out.'

Stephen Covey

READ . . .

TAKE CHARGE

Well done! The hard work has been done now in terms of making changes to your life, but that's not the end of it. You are now at a tipping point in the process, and as you begin the next week of your life, you have three choices which will determine whether or not you live your life with No Regrets on Sunday:

CHOICE 1 – THROW THE BOOK AWAY

You can throw this book and all its guidance away in an instant, rather like switching off a light bulb in your head, and you can simply give up on your ideas, ripping them to pieces before you even start. Our experience at Windmills is that about 15 per cent of all the participants on our programmes fall into this category.

CHOICE 2 – LEAVE IT TO SOME TIME, SOME DAY

Rather than acting on all you have learned now, you can push everything away until later and simply let your ideas sit on a shelf gathering dust, waiting for some time, some day to arrive. In our experience this is where the majority of people on our programmes get stuck – 70 per cent of them are heard to say things like: 'I'll do it when the kids are older ...', 'when I win the lottery ...', 'after the summer holidays ...', 'when I've retired'. They all have an amazing amount of potential but for whatever reason – whether it is confidence, time, self-belief or support – they struggle to follow through and be all they can be. This is just as bad as throwing your hopes away: 'some day' is not a day of the week – it never arrives!

CHOICE 3 – MAINTAIN A HABIT OF A LIFETIME
You could carry on taking really simple and practical actions each day to keep the process going. By bringing your ideas to life and turning them into a daily habit you can make no regrets a way of life. Well done if you are in this category, but again, sadly, our experience shows this tends to only be 15 per cent of those who we come into contact with.

TAKE THE OPPORTUNITY

So, before you decide which option to take, try looking at the following word: OPPORTUNITYISNOWHERE. How do you read it – OPPORTUNITY IS NOWHERE or OPPORTUNITY IS NOW HERE? The word is the same, but depending on your perspective, the meaning is completely different. The same is true of how we look at our future.

Hopefully, as you have worked through this book over the last week a seed of an idea you wish to action or something you may wish to change or consider making happen has been sown in your head. Or maybe you're seeing ideas that you've already planted beginning to grow and blossom. However, like nurturing and caring for plants, trees and shrubs, the key to success lies in how you maintain them. You only have to walk down any street to see how people nurture their plots. However, there are three types of gardens:

1   The garden which has ceased to exist; any possibility for growth has been crushed and overwhelmed by tons of concrete, rubble or waste (Choice 1).

2   Gardens that need a bit of tender loving care. You can see that their owners started with good intentions, but stuff has been left undone or not kept up with. Things have grown out of control and proportion (Choice 2).

3   Finally, there are those fabulously well-kept gardens full of colour, with plants shaped neatly and in proportion to their space and showing exciting signs of new growth (Choice 3).

Which 'garden' sums up your life?

When we've reflected on both our own personal struggles as well as the attempts of thousands of other people to make the most of their lives, have no regrets and take the actions that

> 'Success will never be a big step in the future, success is a small step taken just now.'
>
> **Jonatan Martensson**

are needed, this gardening analogy often comes to mind. Here are 10 top tips to grow and maintain a no regrets habit for life:

1   CULTIVATING FERTILE GROUND

Nobody can expect to throw a seed into rock-solid ground, leave it to the elements and expect it to grow beautifully without any care and attention. From our experience, one of the most crucial conditions for growth is a fertile mindset. Luckily, some people have a predisposition for being optimistic, while others, often due to the environment they grew up in (family, schooling, friends and neighbourhoods) are firmly entrenched in a pessimistic view on life. Some are open, others closed. Some always see the negative in situations; others always look for the positive.

How open are you to positive change?

If you hear yourself saying any of these statements, maybe it's time to do some more groundwork:

- 'I can't do anything about it'
- 'I don't have any choice ...'
- 'I'd love to but ...'
- 'It'll never happen ...'
- 'I couldn't possibly ...'
- 'It's out of my control ...'

Is the ground so fixed, solid and frozen that nothing has the chance to grow, or are you providing rich conditions for growth?

- 'I can'
- 'I will'
- 'Anything's possible'
- 'Let's go for it'
- 'What have we to lose?'

Are you looking forward with a 'frozen' mindset or a 'growth' mindset? The choice is yours!

2 GREENHOUSING SEEDLING IDEAS

Plants are at their most fragile when they are tiny and first emerging through the soil. They need protecting from the elements at this crucial stage of growth, and that is why gardeners in colder climes use greenhouses. It's the same with ideas – they are easiest to kill when they first come to life. Unfortunately, the cultures we live and work in tend to destroy ideas before they take firm root. The winds of change in our lives can also blow our hopes away before they become resilient enough to stand up independently. Each of us dealing with fundamental change in our personal or professional lives needs to protect ourselves in the early stages, otherwise we can become broken. The key is to resist the elements that are out of your control and instead create a more controlled environment – one that you have control over.

To create your own greenhouse you need to:

- Focus on what you can control rather than what you can't.

- Suspend judgement and give things a chance.

- Understand your own fragility and protect yourself from other people's opinions.

- Give things time.

- Nurture positive signs of growth.

- Celebrate every small development.

3 WEEDING OUT THE WORRIES

Like weeds, our worries can quickly grow and before we know it they have tangled themselves around us and choked and smothered our hopes. Some worries are like stinging nettles; they may not instantly affect us but they will raise their ugly head over time, provoking a physical reaction – stress, anxiety, depression and breakdown. Others are like a constant thorn in your side, always nagging away at you and stunting your growth. Some worry weeds also look like flowers, and you get so used to them that you would worry if you didn't have them around you.

As we learned on Monday, 40 per cent of what we worry about never happens, 30 per cent has already happened, 12 per cent focuses on opinions or situations we cannot change, 10 per cent is on our health (which only worsens it), leaving 8 per cent which concerns real problems we can influence. That means that 92 per cent of our worries are absolutely needless! The fascinating thing is that we ourselves nurture and feed our own worries and as a result we have grown them out of all proportion.

Our worries and our hopes are fed by the same thing: our imagination. Our hopes and dreams use imagination in a positive way to create the most colourful, exciting and inspiring vision we can. Our worries and fears use exactly the same imagination to create the darkest, most toxic, worst-case scenario we can imagine. It's not our imagination that affects the outcome, it's how we choose to use it.

So, to help you to make a change in your life, you need to weed out your worries to a point that is manageable and will not prevent you having No Regrets on Sunday:

- Cut out any worries about the past – you can't change what's done, so draw a line and move on.

- Clear out every worry you have in your head and write them down on a piece of paper, then physically dump them all in the recycling bin.

- Check whether your worry is alive or not. Is it simply a figment of your imagination? Where is the evidence – is it just hearsay or have you got real proof?

- Prune out any worries that still remain – take action today to do something positively about any lingering worries.

4 PROCRASTINATING IN THE POT

Procrastination is one of the major barriers to reaching our full potential. Maybe you've grown your life into a good shape –

things aren't blooming but they look okay. You've planted yourself in a nice cosy pot. It's a comfortable environment – you get fed and watered at regular intervals, you're able to stay within your comfort zone and you're well protected from the elements. The danger is that the size of your pot will begin to stunt your growth, but you're so happy in your little comfort zone that you never have the motivation to get repotted. As years – and potentially decades – pass by, self-limiting beliefs continue to prevent any potential growth, which may well lead to regrets when you look back on your life with the benefit of hindsight. You may find yourself thinking: 'I wish I'd done this 10 years earlier', 'if only I'd ...', 'if I could have my time again ...'.

Procrastination comes in many different pots, but they all have one similar feature: they convince you that staying in the same place is for the best.

Can you see yourself or other people in any of these pots?

Honey Pot	Always waiting for the perfect sweet moment. 'I'll do it when I've got enough time, support, energy ...', 'I need to wait until ...', 'I'll do it some day, some time ...'. There is no perfect time, so don't put things off.
Fuss Pot	Constantly fussing about everybody and everything else but not addressing the real issue – themselves: 'I couldn't possibly do it, I've got responsibilities ...', 'I'm the main carer, breadwinner, provider ...', 'work's so busy I haven't got time ...', 'it's all right for other people ...'

Stop fussing around the edges and start to really care for yourself.

Money Pot Money makes the world go around, but the pursuit of it makes your world go even faster. Worrying about it can send your world crashing into the barriers. While we all need money to survive, how much do we truly need to thrive? 'When I've got enough money I'll ...', 'when we win the lottery ...', 'I can only retire when my pension pot is ...'.

The greatest danger here is that money saturates any other factors in making future choices. How much money do you really need to be happy? (Research shows £20k is a breaking point.) Are you prepared to downsize your lifestyle to pursue a meaningful purpose or dream? When planning for retirement have you considered health before finance? The irony is that we are in danger of breaking ourselves in the pursuit of building up a fabulous pension, only to find our health is not good enough to enjoy it. The golden nest egg never hatches.

Hot Pot Here, all the valuable energy is wasted for the wrong purpose. Anger, frustration and annoyance are directed at employers, politicians, specific individuals and everybody else: 'I can't believe that ...', 'management haven't got a clue ...', 'it's their fault ...', 'it's up to them to ...'.

While some of your frustration and anger may be justified, maybe it's time to channel your energy into something more positive and focus on what's in rather than out of your control.

Crack Pot Full of hot air but no real substance. These people have all sorts of grandiose ideas and dreams but are never willing to make them real. Quite random in their nature, they lack the planning and realistic attitude needed to make things happen. For example, we've seen hundreds of graduates who aspire to be journalists but haven't bothered getting any form of work experience using their writing skills. The blockage is not the dream, it's the execution of it – so don't stop dreaming!

Realism is not a barrier to growing your dreams, it is a catalyst which makes them grow real.

Decision time! Are you going to stay in your nice cosy routine and let your life go to pot? Or is it time to replant yourself into a new way of thinking or acting?

'At what age did you conclude that wishes were merely childish things? Who told you to "grow up" and robbed you of your dreams?'

Soure Rushnell

5 CONTROLLING THE PESTS

However well developed our idea, hope or dream, there are always people who can act like common garden pests, taking great delight in eating away at what we are trying to nurture and grow. Some work like an army of ants. These people steal fledgling ideas, working together to loosen the soil around the roots, causing the idea seedling to die before it has even got started. There are also woodlice – people who hide in the undergrowth, waiting for the right time to attack young seedlings and plants. In addition, there are the slugs and snails who slowly eat away at all you've cared for, leaving their trail behind.

The list of pesty bugs is endless. Some attack our core roots and values; others will destroy any hopes as they emerge from the soil. Some will fuel our concerns, others bully us to agree with their beliefs. Even the most attractive and colourful characters, like caterpillars, might enjoy a tasty meal at your expense. We will never get rid of all these pests – that's life – and some of them actually have their uses, keeping us on our toes. So, here are a few tips to keep the pests at bay:

- Avoid places where they congregate (gossip groups in the playground, toxic work environments and negative circles of friends). They will only drag you down and eat away at you.

- Replant yourself into more positive fertile environments, such as a social or work group who share similar values and passions.

- Buy some insecticide and use it promptly and regularly. Have the confidence to stand up for what you believe in, try to understand the purpose behind the actions of these pests, and if you believe there is any hope in changing their behaviour, try to forgive, forget and forge new relationships. Remember, the Greek word for forgiveness means 'letting go'.

6   GROWING YOUR GRAPEVINE

For some people their chances of success can be significantly improved with support from others. They need a framework or solid structure on which to grow. They need their own personal gardener to talk to them, place them in the right environment, feed and water them and help them branch out in new directions. Like a good wine, the quality of the grape is dependent on the quality of the grapevine, which in turn is dependent on the quality of its support framework and root system.

To really bear fruit in life we cannot act alone; you only have to look at how nature works in our gardens to realise the truth of this. Bees collect and transfer pollen; birds recycle vegetation; the wind enables seeds to be pollinated; worms cultivate soil; and fallen apples provide energy for families of insects. While our gardens may be walled or fenced off, we are all interconnected in some way.

So how good is your grapevine/support network? Do you have a trusted platform on which to grow and flourish? If not, here are a few ideas to develop it:

- Find an experienced gardener, a coach or a mentor who can help you.

- Invest in an allotment plot – buddy up with someone else, a friend, family member or some colleagues, and enjoy sowing a few seeds together.

- Visit the garden centre – gain a wider network of support and advice.

- Build a trellis – take time out to create a secure support framework, battening down all the willing people who can help train you in the right direction.

- Learn about 'the birds and the bees' – those people who can spread the word and transport you to different places.

- Hang around on the south-facing slopes where there is warmth – very little grows on the shadows of the north-facing sites.

'If we are facing in the right direction, all we have to do is keep on walking.'

Buddhist saying

- Go to the place that produces the best wine in the world – in other words, find someone who is the best in your field or doing something you've always dreamed of doing and learn from their story.

7 CREEPING IN THE RIGHT DIRECTION

Like plants that need the sun and rain to grow, we too need the right combination of elements. People are either 'pulled' and naturally attracted towards something really exciting and meaningful for them (the sun), or 'pushed' away because the environment they're in has reached saturation point (the rain). However, many of us find ourselves without enough sun or rain. Things aren't so bad at work, home or in our social life that we are forced to make a change, but also we haven't got a vision that is clear or desirable enough for us to make the effort required to reach it.

We are in limbo, never really reaching our full potential. So how bad does it have to get before you do something about it? As one client said, 'I knew when it was time to change when I became sick and tired of saying how sick and tired I was about the situation.' The danger with this 'breaking point' approach is you are taking action in a potentially unresourceful state – poor conditions have rotted your confidence, while torrential pressure, change and uncertainty has swamped you, and as a result you feel absolutely saturated.

In the worst-case scenarios, like expensive tropical plants left out in pots during a harsh winter, their soil becomes saturated, then frozen in the cold weather and they die. It's a fact that work, stress and financially related breakdowns and suicides are on the increase. Similarly, a new group of residents occupying beds in mental health wards are highly professional people who are unable to 'switch off' from work challenges and worries and the overload has caused a power cut. We all have different tolerance levels, but you need to decide when enough is enough before letting it get out of hand.

A far more inspiring role model is a colourful character that pops up occasionally to brighten us up on our travels – the sunflower. At every opportunity, towards the sun it creeps, slowly yet purposefully stretching to something it will never reach but gaining warmth, energy and direction from this higher goal. The end point is worth aiming for. So how good does it have to be for you to have the desire and determination to move towards it? You may not have to reach the dizzy heights or achieve some higher goal, but score your ideas and plans out of 10 in terms of motivation (0 = totally unmotivating, 10 = it's amazing, I'm going to do it now). If, for example, you scored a 4, what needs to be in place to make it a 7, and at 7 what would bring it closer to a 10?

> 'Any idiot can face a crisis – it's day-to-day living that wears you out.'
>
> **Anton Chekhov**

We don't have any problems chasing the sun for a two-week holiday, so how are you going to bring more warmth and happiness into the other 50 weeks of your year? Like the sunflower, you don't have to make massive changes; all you need to do is creep in the right direction.

8 PLANTING A LEGACY

One major frustration that people have when trying to make change happen is the time it takes to do so. You can't plant an acorn in the ground and expect an oak tree within a week, no matter how much you care for it.

People get frustrated with how long it takes to find a new job, develop new clients, buy a new home and develop lifelong friendships. It's fairly cheap and easy to buy ready-grown seasonal bedding plants, but they only provide colour and interest for short periods of time, and larger, more attractive shrubs, bushes and trees are extremely expensive to buy fully grown.

Our hopes and dreams take time to mature before they can truly flourish, yet in a time of instant gratification we are not prepared to wait. Like plants, it's also really expensive, if not impossible, to buy established businesses, ready-grown qualifications, high-quality homes or deep-rooted charities. It's far cheaper to grow your own.

But it's not all about growing things for your own consumption – how about planting your own legacy? Something that will be there when you leave this life.

At Windmills we were privileged enough to evaluate the lessons learned by change agents in a £60-million Government initiative that attempted to make long-term improvements in the way young people are prepared for life. Their experience of mastering (and mistressing) change is summarised in the following ACORN principle.

Action	Create an early win, an activity or a project that demonstrates in a small way the change you wish to make.
Communication	Develop a clear strategy for telling people about the benefits of your idea.
Ownership	Find champions – people who are influential and interested enough to support your idea, and grow robust, trusting relationships with them so they feel a level of ownership.
Reflection	Build in quality time for reflection, asking yourself whether it's making a difference, taking you and others in the right direction and matching your values and strengths. Be responsive to any lessons learned.
Nurture	Embed the change, focusing on the roots rather than the branches, putting in place the appropriate practices, people, policies, processes and partnerships needed to feed and maintain future growth.

So what small acorns are you going to plant today with patience and care to benefit yourself, those you love and the wider community tomorrow?

'The greatest oak tree was once a little nut that held its ground.'

Unknown

9 GETTING YOUR HANDS DIRTY

Having the right tools and equipment for gardening will always make the job easier. As we get older, choosing them wisely is even more important. It sometimes means the difference between doing a task and not.

The same goes with our life – we all need our personal tool kit to control and shape it to the way we want it to be ultimately. Each of us will have our own requirements but certain equipment will be crucial.

We all need our spades (self-awareness) to dig deep enough to understand the real roots of what's important to us, and find our hidden strengths and treasures. Forks and hoes (exploring skills) are crucial to uncover new opportunities and sow new possibilities. Without the right shears, secateurs and saws (decision-making tools) it will be hard to cut back areas of our life, such as work, which may be growing out of control, overshadowing everything else and not enabling other important things to have life. And without the wheelbarrow and rubbish bin how can we transplant and recycle things or even put our failures, rejections and rotten situations on to the compost heap of life to be broken down and wisely re-used to feed new growth in the future?

Without careful maintenance our tools will lack sharpness and soon become rusty. If our tools are blunt it leaves us vulnerable to letting someone else cut us down with a negative comment or unsettle the foundations of a new idea. Similarly, if they're not left in a safe place, our tools may get into the wrong hands and become dangerous.

At the end of the day, you need to get your hands dirty and take some positive action. This book gives you all the tools you need, but it's up to you to maintain them. If you hear yourself saying 'I'm too old ...', ask yourself, 'Too old for what?' If you feel 'it's too risky to do something', ask yourself, 'What's the risk if I don't?' If you're worried about what other people will think, stop worrying. If you're focusing on what you're not capable of, try highlighting what you are capable of instead.

> 'It is one of the paradoxes of success that the things and ways which get you there are seldom those things that keep you there.'
>
> **Charles Handy**

Choose the tools that are appropriate for you at each stage of your life. A young workman may need a different size and weight of spade than an elderly lady, so you may need to revisit and put different weights on to each exercise as your working, learning, playing and giving grow together.

10 VEGGING OUT

As our lives unfold and accommodate change, so do our gardens. Ponds may be replaced by football pitches and vice versa, vegetable plots sprout up over waste ground, budding climbing plants grow around climbing frames, hedges and fences erected to provide boundaries between different areas, and the ground opened up to bury the much-loved guinea pig, rabbit or cat. We may even end up scattered among the roses ourselves!

Although each of us has different approaches to both our gardens and our lives, we can be in danger of not appreciating them fully. We may never enjoy the present moment because we are always toiling for the next big thing. We don't appreciate what we do have because we are spending all our time focusing on what we don't have.

There is therefore a fine balance between picturing the destination and enjoying the journey. Or maybe, with Tuesday's learning in mind, it's about blending the two together and being mindful of both the bigger and smaller picture. One thing is clear: it's not all about having or doing, it's about being – and this requires simply vegging out at times and being grateful for what is around you, what you've achieved so far, who has helped with your development and looking forward with care and hopeful anticipation to new seeds of growth.

To conclude, you have choices over your future. Are you going to concrete it over, leave it to grow out of control or maintain the great investment you've already made? Are you going to come up smelling of roses or be a thorn in your own side? The choice is yours.

'If not now, when?
If not you, who?
Give yourself permission
to be all you can be.'

Ken Pye

THINK...

THE NO REGRETS CHECKLIST OF 20 TOP TIPS

The following checklist is intended to help you maintain the process. They may stimulate ways of keeping your momentum going if you are struggling. Simply tick any ideas you feel both make a difference and are something you feel motivated enough to achieve. Feel free to add your own ideas to the list.

1 **Break habits** – go to work a different way, listen to a new radio station or buy a different paper. Go to places you wouldn't normally visit: join a new group, turn off the TV and do something different.

2 **Bring in help** – use your contacts and find someone who inspires you or has been through the same experience as you. Write down specifically what you want their support with and phone them up and learn from their experiences.

3 **Boost your well-being** – develop a healthy body and mindset. Exercise by walking instead of driving and try making steps to eating a healthier diet. Be positive by celebrating all you have achieved so far and using this to build resilience when worry and anxiety take over.

4 **Begin with the end in mind** – imagine a happy end to your day/week/month/year/life. You've no regrets; you've made a real difference yet had loads of fun. Start the day with that attitude and stick to the plan.

5 **Talk about WLPG** – speak to one person who is affected by your WLPG. Ask them to draw their own sketch. See how you can work together to help each other.

6 **Learn to learn** – find something you'd love to learn and build it into your day, whether formally through a programme of study or informally, taking every opportunity to learn from others.

7 **Work to live** – research ways in which you can find more flexible work to fund your passions, support your learning or free you up to give more. Use an interview for information, pinpointing someone doing what you'd love to do and asking if they can spare you a few minutes.

8 **Remember your most important role** – playing a leadership role in your own life will make sure you create what's right for you. Take one small action to take a greater level of control of what you are doing instead of letting it happen. By doing this you can share your experience by helping others to do the same.

9 **Understand your roles** – recognise what they mean to others. Ask family and friends, 'How can I be a better neighbour, colleague or friend … in your eyes?'

10 **Get your priorities right** – focus energy on things that really matter. Postpone the routine day job stuff that will still be there tomorrow and spend quality time with friends. Take some time and surprise your parents with a visit.

11 **Keep checking** – reassure yourself you're making progress but keep checking that you are moving in the right direction in the right way for the right reasons, and for what you want to achieve.

12 **Focus on strengths** – believe in the skills you're really good at and use these wherever and whenever you can. Find one activity that uses one or two skills you love using most and are really good at. Sacrifice TV time to help a friend develop IT skills, or volunteer to design a newsletter for a charity.

13 **Stretch your comfort zone** – take on the next challenge: it may take months or years to achieve it, but start now.

14 **Volunteer your time and talents** – giving your time and talent to causes that matter to you lets you put things in perspective and appreciate what you already have.

15 **Create more 'me time'** – diarise some quality time for yourself and refuse to feel guilty about relaxing. If you are not feeling resourceful for yourself you will not be able to help others.

16 **Choose your mood** – whatever happens, you always have a choice to feel as you are feeling – remind yourself of this when your mood is less than positive. Don't wait for the 'right' time/place or situation to feel better. Dump those negative thoughts and simply enjoy yourself.

17 **Start a new chapter** – imagine your Golden Ticket is a book. List chapter headings, write page one and begin to act it out. You're in charge of the characters, plot and how it ends.

18 **Develop different scenarios** – try creating many different versions of your Golden Ticket. Vary the time or scale of your ambitions. Start with a manageable vision, add bolder ideas then review each version.

19 **Boost your luck** – learn the art of speaking to strangers – in the supermarket queue, the bus or train, etc. Just asking 'How has your day been?' might work as an ice-breaker.

20 **Be honest** – confront your obstacles. If it's time or commitment, question what's really stopping you. If it's money, see what savings you can make that will make it possible for you to earn less and avoid 'W' dominating your life.

'Take care of your body,
it's the only place you have to live.'
Jim Rohn

ACT...

THE NO REGRETS WEEKLY PLANNER

To maintain the no regrets way of life it's important to make it into a habit from the outset.

1   Review the ideas you've ticked in the No Regrets Checklist above and pick one action per day that will keep the process going.

2   Use the simple weekly planner opposite to highlight the specific actions you're committing to on each day of the week. Place these in Column 1. If you need any further inspiration have a look at what other people have done as part of this process. These 101 ideas can be found on page 201.

3   As you progress through each action, reflect on what you've learned and anything that surprises or puzzles you. You may also highlight new actions you need to take as a result. Log all this information in Column 2.

4   Try to complete this exercise for the next two or three weeks using the remaining actions from the 'think' section, or possibilities that have arisen from what you've achieved so far.

5   Over time, you may not need to write down your actions and reflections – they should become a daily habit.

NO REGRETS WEEKLY PLANNER

DAY	ACTION (The action I'm going to take)	REFLECTION (What I've learned, what puzzles me, future actions)
MONDAY		
TUESDAY		
WEDNESDAY		
THURSDAY		
FRIDAY		
SATURDAY		
SUNDAY		

It's now time to be all you can be – if you don't, who will?

'Don't judge each day by the harvest
you reap but by the seeds that you plant.'
Robert Louis Stevenson

conclusion

To end this book I'd like to share with you one of my favourite stories about a little boy playing on a beach. On his travels along the shore the boy comes across hundreds of starfish washed up on the sand. The tide is going out fast, leaving the starfish to die in the hot baking sun. The trapped starfish lie helplessly awaiting their fate, in a trail stretching right along the coastline as far as the eye can see. The little boy begins to bend down to pick one up, when he feels a firm hand on his shoulder. An older man has appeared from nowhere and in a rather gruff, condescending voice says, 'What's the point of trying to save them? Don't be stupid, there are too many. You'll never make a difference,' to which the little boy replies, as he eagerly picks up the first starfish and throws it back into the sea, 'Well, that made a difference to this one,' and 'That made a difference to another one', as the second plopped into the water. The little boy looks up excitedly. 'Will you help me please, sir?' And the man did! They didn't save every starfish, but together they made their own small difference.

However great your task or the challenge ahead, it's better to do something rather than nothing. We may only be as small as a grain of sand on the beach, but we can make a lasting impact, especially if we work together. You now have your own personal tool kit to a no regrets way of life. So our final challenge to you is simple: *To play your part and never believe that you can't make a difference.*

Give yourself permission to be all you can be. You are a special, unique person with all sorts of hidden talents. You owe it to yourself to live your life to its full potential and script your own future. Stop instantly making those reasonable excuses why it's impossible to do things. Life is not a dress rehearsal, so start believing in yourself: if you don't who will? And, remember, your mindset will make the difference between a good and great day. Focus on what really matters to you.

MAKE IT HAPPEN

Try not to be overwhelmed by the enormity of your ideas. Now that you have completed the seven days, the promise of the future and what you have discovered about yourself might seem overwhelming. Stay calm and focus on the big picture, while building towards it in small steps. You have accumulated some great new tools to define who you want to be and what is important in your life – keep your personal EATing habits, your WLPG charts, your Skills Portfolio, your Golden Ticket and everything else close to hand – look at them often and use them to inspire you and to rise above the clamour of everyday life. Another great habit that you have gained this past week is to find some time every day to think about your life and how to make it and yourself better and happier. Make sure that you continue with this – try to ensure that you take even just 15 minutes each day to put aside everything else and concentrate on you and where you want to go in life.

BIG CHANGES COME FROM LITTLE STEPS

Take lots of baby steps. Again don't feel daunted by the task at hand. The best way to eat an elephant is a mouthful at a time. So make that phone call, commit to the course you've put off for ages, arrange that meeting with the boss and visit that elderly neighbour you haven't seen for ages. Every book starts with a first line, so what's your new chapter going to start with?

'A journey of a thousand miles begins with a single step.'

Lao Tzu

Here are some prompts to help you remember the steps you need to take to leading an inspiring life:

MONDAY – MINDSET

How can you act and think differently today? Look at your EATing habits and choose the one that makes you uncomfortable. For one day – act completely against character and defy your fears to make a change. You can be whatever you want to be, don't let you stop yourself from reaching towards your dream future. Remember that if you had the courage to pick up and read this book and recognise what needs to change, then you have the courage to follow it through.

TUESDAY – TIME

Who do you need to have more fun with, give more time to or simply be with today? Don't slip back into bad habits and let your daily life overwhelm you. Now that you have found one hour each day this past week – continue this habit. And keep looking at your WLPG charts and checking that you are moving forward and bringing more fulfilment and satisfaction into every hour of your life.

WEDNESDAY – WHO

Who do you feel like being today? Remember that you must be true to yourself to achieve your best in life and to be the most fulfilled. You will have the strength and energy to give to the most important roles that you inhabit if you find the time that you need for yourself first.

THURSDAY – TALENTS

Think of a talent that you've always dreamt of pursuing but have never taken steps towards. Do something crazy and try something completely new. If you don't enjoy it or it doesn't work out then it doesn't actually matter, but don't always play the safe option. This is your time to try skydiving, learn a musical instrument or travel to the other side of the world. Pushing against those comfort barriers helps create new pathways in the brain and new ways of thinking, and brings much greater rewards than just new experiences to your life.

FRIDAY – FULFILMENT

Choose a passion that you have that makes you happy and make it work for you and those around you. Be brave and step into the limelight and push yourself forward. Sharing your passions with others is a wonderful way of giving to others and yourself at the same time – it's an easy win.

SATURDAY – SATISFACTION

Tell whoever you meet that will listen about your plans and what you want to achieve. Spread the word – it will not only inspire you to push yourself forward at every opportunity, it will also guarantee that you will find ways and people who can help you turn your dreams into reality. Don't be shy – announce your plans to the world.

SUNDAY – SUPPORT

Don't worry if you can't do everything by yourself. You've already got an amazing supporting cast. Don't be afraid to ask for help, whether it be people to hold your hand and walk with you, give you a gentle push or prod, point you in the right direction or simply give you a hug when you feel low. And it's really exciting and comforting to know that when you do put yourself on to new stages there are all sorts of wonderful new people waiting in the wings to play their part and have fun with you.

TIME TO START A NEW CHAPTER

Imagine just before you pass away, you enter a house and go into the library. Here, a person such as Morgan Freeman appears from nowhere and presents you with a book – the book of your life. It contains the complete truth – everything good and bad that has happened in your life, even the bits you thought nobody would know about. He's read it and congratulates you on it, but then he asks you a few questions ... 'Tell me, why did you spend so long in Chapter 5 working in that boring, laborious job you hated, and what was the reason for waiting until Chapter 15 before you spent some quality time on yourself? Why did you spend those 100 pages worrying about something that never happened? Why did you make the lives of your fellow travellers a misery by constantly moaning about things you could have solved yourself? Why in Chapter 17 did you say you were going to change your life, but in the next sentence made an excuse why this was not possible?'

Just before he disappears he adds one final comment. 'You know that one liner on page 362, when you listened to that stranger on the train? Well, that changed the next three chapters of their book too! In fact hundreds of one liners in your book have changed the plot of thousands of other people who in turn have influenced millions of other books.'

Today the book of your life is only partially written. You, now at this very moment, have a magical opportunity to create a fresh new chapter and write those one liners. Please don't give the responsibility to someone else or expect someone else to make your dreams come true for you. You'll never be able to control what they write. Your future is literally in your own hands. Here are a few final words to help you on your way.

> 'A goal without a plan is just a wish.'
>
> **Antoine de Saint-Exupery**

EMBRACE CHANGE AND HAVE COURAGE

The biggest decision that you can take from this book is to make the big changes that you need to make in your life for it to be truly special. By all means, take baby steps towards your end dream, but never lose sight of where you are aiming. If jumping off that cliff is the only way to make the major changes that need to be made, then you know that you have the courage to do it.

It's not the number of times you get knocked down that matters, it's the number of times you get back up that counts, so stop being paralysed by fear of failure and start tackling the important stuff head-on. However fit you are to play the game of life, it's only possible to score a goal when you are on the pitch. So don't stand there passively watching life go by: get stuck in and give it your best shot.

TAKE ACTION NOW

Finally, please don't leave your seven-day plan gathering dust on the shelf. You now have a simple structure to take control of your destiny but it's over to you to make it happen. Keep revisiting each chapter and regularly check whether you're heading in the right direction. Try to apply the lessons you've learned to every aspect of your life and share them with the people who really matter to you. Please don't get to the last page of your book saying 'I wish I had ...'

At the end of this week now we are not going to wish you good luck – because you don't need it, you'll create your own. But to truly reap the rewards of all your hard work during the week, please continue to take small brave steps today and every day to have No Regrets on Sunday.

'The best way to predict your future is to create it.'

Unknown

101 ways to have No Regrets on Sunday

Below are 101 simple things people have done each day to put no regrets into practice. You may find one simple action or thought stimulates a new idea in your own life.

MONDAY: MINDSET

- Nothing has changed but I've just started to look at things differently.

- I've arranged to meet with a more positive colleague every month to keep me on track.

- I've stopped worrying about what other mums in the playground think of me.

- I've recognised that I am choosing to think and behave in a certain way, so I've given myself permission to change.

- I've started to focus on all the good things in work instead of slipping into the normal negative response.

- I chose to have a go at diving, which I've never done before, to boost my 'curiosity' score – which was my lowest.

- I've simply said 'no' more, which freed up more time to do what I really wanted to do.

- I asked a couple of friends to score me on the 10 c's (see pages 10–11). They scored me higher than I did which really boosted my confidence.

- I listed all my worries and chose to stop worrying about them.

- I agreed with my wife that we wouldn't discuss work problems at home.

- I walked to school a different way to break my routine.

- I listed all the things I was grateful for in my current job and realised I wouldn't have them if I jumped ship.

- I chose to believe in myself more. If I don't, who will?

- I realised I've been procrastinating in the public sector for the past 27 years and took the plunge into an exciting new business venture.

TUESDAY: TIME

- I started using the words WLPG more – I've started using this in our department so it's now entered into our vocabulary.

- I carry my ideal blend of WLPG circles in my wallet so I can keep thinking about it much more.

- I discussed my WLPG blend with my husband and developed one for us both.

- I used the holiday we had planned to grow my learning, which was my smallest circle, and planned visits and activities to actively do this.

- I got my wife to draw out how she saw my WLPG. I realised I was learning more than I thought.

- I used a box to represent time I have left in my life and tried to cram four balloons in which represented my WLPG circles. It helped to get my kids to think about which is most important to them and what should go in first.

- I explained the four circles to a friend at the bar, using spilt beer to draw them.

- I plucked up courage to leave the board meeting earlier and see my daughter in her school play.

- I researched fine art and photography courses at the local college.

- I gave four balls of coloured string to colleagues and asked them to create their own circles on the floor, getting them to step into each area and talk through their WLPG.

- I stopped coming into work on Sundays and went to the gym instead.

- I posed a question to a friend asking them what they'd do if they lost their W circle.

- I left my full-time job and created a portfolio of paid and unpaid work.

- I volunteered to do some gardening at a local residential home close to my heart.

WEDNESDAY: WHO

- I started the discussion among my group of girlfriends about how we support one another and if the things I feel I don't do well are a problem for them or not. I felt relieved and clearer about what I do for them and what they do for me.

- I used the roles activity as a chance to talk to my daughter about whether I could be a better mum, and from this reassured her that she needn't beat herself up about always being there for me.

- I recognised that a major role was going to be disappearing in the next few months so thought about potential new roles. I became a governor in a disadvantaged school and set up my own sewing business.

- I'm now a parent 'from a distance' instead of being in the same location as my children on a full-time basis. I had a chat with them about what support they felt they needed going forward.

- I took my mum on holiday to America.

- Knowing that in the restructure my work role was going, I asked my manager to help me look for other roles in the business that more closely matched my skills and passions.

- As a result of a spontaneous shopping trip with my sister she offered to look after the children so I could have some 'me' time.

- I went out cycling with my nephews.

- I planned to spend an hour of quality time with my son each day for a week. I managed 5 out of 7 days.

- I texted an old friend I'd lost touch with and went out for coffee with them.

- I sat down and watched TV for half an hour with my daughter – something I never do.

- I bought a new house with my boyfriend.

- I took my husband out for pie and chips.

- I went to my son's sports day for the first time in five years.

- I negotiated a term-time contract so I could spend more time on my role as a mother.

THURSDAY: TALENTS

- I resigned from an unfulfilling role and have decided to retrain for midwifery.

- I used my skills in working with groups to increase my giving in the community by setting up a theatre group.

- I re-awakened my interest in Indie music and subscribed to a new magazine, listened to a new radio station I've found on digital radio and got tickets for a couple of concerts later in the year.

- I am committed to finishing off my financial qualifications.

- I played the piano again – the first time for over 10 years.

- I used my design skills (which I don't manage to use as creatively in work as I'd like) to help a friend set up a new website for his business.

- I gained the confidence to update my CV and secured an ideal marketing job.

- I realised my 'networking' skills had decreased when I did the exercise again so made sure I got out and about more in work.

- I highlighted the top 15 companies I'd like to work for and prepared a pitch that would show each the benefits I could bring.

- I saw a gap in housing service provision and put a proposal to my boss.

- I was lacking so much confidence I couldn't even do the exercise, so I agreed to ask five trusted friends to list what they felt were my strengths.

- I'm an accountant but realised I love coaching people, so I volunteered to help at the local kids' football team.

- I retired early from the Navy and completed an occupational therapy degree.

- I went and had a frank and open discussion with my line manager which helped clear the air.

FRIDAY: FULFILMENT

- I used my passion for reading to train as a reading group facilitator and support individuals suffering with addiction and mental health issues.

- I started talking to those in my community about setting up a charity shop to benefit local community initiatives.

- I am going back to Africa for a month to work on a project that I've had a connection with for years, but haven't visited since I qualified, to pass my nursing skills on to others.

- I am going to career change to train as a teacher to do something I feel is more meaningful than insurance.

- I have contacted a group of friends who all share a passion in music to start practising as a band to play at local charity gigs.

- I have teamed up with some old friends to produce a short film.

- I utilised my marketing skills to raise public awareness of people-trafficking.

- I gave blood.

- I built a school in Africa.

- I have started a Spanish class.

- I decided to go back to an old hobby – making cards and crafts – and have set up my own little business.

- I've always loved food and cooking and have now taken the plunge to set up my cake-baking business.

- I set up a debt counselling service in my local church.

- I enrolled on an environmental studies Open University degree.

- I secured an internal secondment moving from waste management to supporting at-risk children, a real passion of mine.

SATURDAY: SATISFACTION

- I created a whole family Golden Ticket, then shared it collectively and we all began to work on key aspects. We're going to do this each year.

- I'm going to laminate my Golden Ticket and put it up on my wall to check my progress.

- I've joined forces with a couple of other friends and families to set up a charity that empowers young people to realise their full potential.

- I decided to share my vision for the future with my friends – after all, they are part of it too – and ask them to help me achieve it.

- I took the chance to discuss my aspirations with my employer who agreed to a sabbatical for three months. I returned feeling valued and even more committed.

- I put all my eggs in one basket and focused on an internal job opportunity. Luckily, I got it!

- I have just celebrated all I've achieved over the last year and I decided to create an annual photo-book online as a permanent record of my journey.

- I spent a night in with my partner, opened a bottle of wine and talked about our joint plans.

- I sat down with two business partners to discuss our own personal hopes for the future.

- I got three generations of my family together for a day and we all shared our Golden Tickets.

- My wife and I decided to create a collective mosaic of what we wanted our future to be using pictures and words from old magazines. With one space left we had to decide between my wife's fast car or my image representing health. She conceded that you can't buy health!

- I stuck my Golden Ticket to the fridge so I'd see it every day.

- My partner and I have decided to run a bed and breakfast on the south-west coast.

- It has challenged me to create an even bigger vision for my family advocacy charity.

- I've moved to France as a direct result of my Golden Ticket.

SUNDAY: SUPPORT

- I've stopped writing Christmas cards that say 'we must get together' and rung three old friends to arrange a meet-up.

- I recognised that some of the people in work are those who 'pull me down'. I made an effort to broaden the people that I chat with and sit with at lunch so I can change the negative script to a more positive one.

- I felt quite lonely so I got involved in a walking group to meet new people in a pastime I love doing.

- I have been brave enough at work to talk to a colleague I met on a recent project to volunteer to work with them again, because he was a great role model.

- I have created a photo frame of all those that support me to celebrate all I have. I am now doing one for those I support – it's a pleasure to look at both of them.

- I've found a chief motivator, someone who knows me well but is prepared to push me and make sure I do what I say I'll do.

- I asked my children whether they thought I was happy at work – they said no!

- Rather than solving my team's problems I've encouraged them to solve their own.

- It was a shock to be made redundant, but the best thing I ever did was to map out everyone I knew. I forgot an old school friend had just set up his own advice business and he needed an extra pair of hands.

- I told my mum how much I loved her.

- For the first time I swallowed my pride and asked for help.

- By volunteering to help people worse off than me, I've realised how lucky I am. It's given me a new sense of purpose and a real kick up the backside.

- It gave me the confidence to register on an online dating agency and I am now in a new relationship.

- I've now got a buddy to go through the change process with. We are both far more resilient working together.

If this is an inspiration to you, then tell us your story or what you have done today to start changing your life. Contact us at www.facebook.com/noregretsonsunday.

about the author

DR PETER HAWKINS IS A CO-DIRECTOR OF WINDMILLS. WITH HIS FAMILY AT THE HEART OF HIS LIFE, HE CREATIVELY BLENDS HIS WORKING, LEARNING, PLAYING AND GIVING.

WORKING – Through Windmills, Peter is an international expert on career and life management. He is the author of seven books, including the acclaimed *The Art of Building Windmills*. Working with Windmills enables Peter to engage in the triple bottom line of work/life balance, making a difference and being paid to pursue his passions. Peter is privileged to work with an amazing and diverse community of like-minded individuals who share similar values and have a warm heart. His vision for Windmills is to invent new ways to inspire people to take control, live their dreams and leave their unique legacy in the world.

LEARNING – An engineering graduate with a passion for people development, Peter has a PhD in Industrial Management. Over the past 20 years he has lectured across the world from Harvard to Cape Town Universities as an international expert on career and life management. He is an NLP Master Practitioner and has been mentored by inspirational leaders including Charles Handy and Dick Bolles.

PLAYING – Although registered blind, his numerous sporting challenges include cycling from Land's End to John O'Groats, running the London Marathon and walking the Three Peaks – all for charities close to his heart. Based in Formby, 15 miles up the coast from Liverpool, Peter always enjoys 'Fun Fridays' with his family. His freedom and flexibility of work patterns allow him to drop off and pick up his boys from school and be an active part of the local community.

GIVING – Peter is passionate about empowering people with special needs. As leader and trustee for the Thursday Club, a charity for adults with learning difficulties, he has acted as an advocate, befriender and helper for over 50 members and their families over the past 25 years. He is also Chair of Governors for a Toxteth-based special needs school and volunteers regularly to speak at various educational and community-based events. With like-minded partners, Peter has been instrumental in establishing the Windmills Foundation Charity, of which he is a trustee.

about windmills

'When the wind blows, some people build walls, others build windmills.'

Windmills was established over 15 years ago as a department of The University of Liverpool, committed to researching issues of personal development and devising practical resources to realise the potential of individuals, organisations and the wider community. Now an independent limited company and a charity, our commitment to cutting-edge research and pragmatic development is still at the heart of the organisation. As a value-based organisation with a social agenda we endeavour to 'be all we can be' by operating under the values of being: 'creative, collaborative, giving, trustworthy, enthusiastic and brave'.

Dr Peter Hawkins and Helen Wakefield are co-directors and have worked on developing the extended Windmills family of clients and partners since the start. They are supported by a dedicated and passionate team of colleagues who together with them 'practise what they preach' in the work they do and the partnerships they create.

Utilising innovative thinking and market-leading resources, Windmills develops resources and programmes for individuals and organisations, creating tailored solutions which maximise personal potential, enhance organisational growth and encourage community development. Supporting people at differing stages in their life, Windmills works with those seeking to resolve work/life balance issues, and helping them to handle career development and change.

The Windmills portfolio helps support individuals, organisations and communities on issues ranging from career and talent management, volunteering and employee engagement, organisational development and retirement planning through to maximising personal potential.

Satisfied clients and partners have come from the public, private and third sectors including Shell, KPMG, Avviva, 02, The Open University and various Hospital Trusts and Deaneries.

The continued development of the portfolio to provide cutting-edge and innovative solutions for individual and business issues is at the heart of Windmills' activity. Windmills has developed a champions programme which equips individuals within organisations with the tools and techniques to cascade the portfolio across their own client groups.

More information on Windmills can be found at
www.windmillsonline.co.uk

the windmills foundation

Are you looking to make a difference in the world? The Windmills Foundation is a charity committed to inspiring young people to make the world a better place. The charity helps young people with the passion, energy and vision to realise their full potential and make a positive contribution to their wider community. We seek to collaborate with like-minded individuals and organisations to develop a new generation of young people who think beyond themselves and play their part in building a more inspiring future.

To realise this ambition, the Windmills Foundation empowers individuals, supports projects and develops partnerships to enable young people to be the best they can be. We are extremely keen to work with individuals, organisations or associations who are committed to each of these three aims:

- Releasing the enormous potential of young people aged 25 and under

- Making a difference to a real community need

and

- Creating trusting, collaborative relationships with like-minded partners who share common values and visions.

We are hoping to make more young people smile by:

Sharing	Passing on their skills, talents, passions and hopes to others.
Meaningful	Focusing on something that really matters to them and their wider community.
Impact	Creating a positive difference in the world based on their unique skills and passions.
Legacy	Making it stick and last over time, not just a one-off wonder.
Enjoyable	Connecting with others (families, friends, schools, neighbours, employers, charities, community and faith groups) in a fun way to make a greater difference than they would by themselves.

We are currently working with seven primary schools, two secondary schools, a politician, Save the Children, local small businesses and parents to deliver the Windmills £10 Challenge. Each year 500 ten and eleven year olds are given £10 to make the world a better place. Their goal is to make people SMILE, but they cannot give the £10 to anybody else: in small groups they have to combine their skills, talents and passions to make a lasting difference in the community. The results have been amazing.

If you are interested in the £10 challenge or being part of the Windmills Foundation, we'd love to hear from you. Please visit, www.windmillsonline.co.uk or contact us at foundation@windmillsonline.co.uk.

acknowledgements

They say a smile goes a long way, but open arms go a lot further. Thanks a million to all those who have so freely offered a helping hand in creating *No Regrets on Sunday*. Without your help, advice and encouragement this book would not be here today.

Special thanks go to two Helens in my life. My wife Helen, whose belief and love has been amazing throughout all the highs and lows. And my business partner Helen whose shared vision and values, together with her complementary skills, have made no regrets a reality.

I am extremely lucky and privileged to have been mentored by two extraordinary characters – Charles Handy and Dick Bolles who have both inspired me to think about and live life in radically new ways.

A massive thank you goes to all my friends and colleagues at Windmills, in particular Colin, Sharon, Jason, Lynne, Brian, Gill, Ritchie, Iain, Ruth and Tim as well as the hundreds of clients who have freely offered their case studies, stories and feedback.

And to the Thursday Club and Princes Primary School for being such an inspiration.

Without the support, encouragement and flexibility of our families we would not be celebrating this publication today.

Special thanks go to Phil, Sarah and Joe Wakefield for their unquestioning enthusiasm and back-up.

The ideas in this book could not be passed on to you without the publishing expertise at Random House. Thank you Susanna and your team for believing in me, and Helena and Kate for providing a fresh perspective. A big thanks also goes to all the 'invisible people' who have played their unique part in bringing this book to you – from designers, publicists, proof readers and printers to the booksellers.

Finally, to my Mum and Dad, Pat and Colin, who are simply my best friends.